Global Cause Marketing

Future-Proof Your Brand

By Peter L Hirsch
and
Robert B Gordon

Praise for *Global Cause Marketing*

Corporate social responsibility works when it is deeply ingrained in the culture and highly connected to the strategy of a company. This is not easy to do, but pays huge rewards for both the company, and society over the long term. *Global Cause Marketing* provides a game-plan for any company -- whether big or small – to make this happen.

-- Matt Flannery, Co-founder and CEO, Kiva

The Principles *Global Cause Marketing* teaches will help you get the most out of life and work. The future of business is headed in this direction and I suggest you get on board.

-- Vicente Fox, President of Mexico, 2000-2006

As I watch the next generation of consumers evolve it is so very apparent that there is a significantly increased interest is developing brand loyalty toward brands/companies that have a conscience. *Global Cause Marketing* captures the essence of this movement and shines a light on understanding the how's and why's. It's a great thought piece as well as a fantastic practical tool.

-- Dan Zigulich, VP, Global Creative Marketing, Payless ShoeSource

This is a practical guide that demonstrates that success – and significance – is measured as much by what we contribute to the world around us as by what we gain in money, titles and belongings.

-- Sam Caster, Founder, Mannatech and MannaRelief

Peter and Bob have opened the door for thousands of people to enter into success. They will inspire you to live every day with passion as you embrace your purpose.

-- Dr. John C. Maxwell, Founder, The INJOY Group

Peter and Bob show us how to let go, and let God change the meaning of our lives by design, rather than delusion.

-- Dr. Denis Waitley, Author, Seeds of Greatness

Peter and Bob's teachings are stimulating and inspiring. They will encourage and excite you to the point of action.

-- Rudy Ruettiger, Inspiration behind the film, Rudy

It's time for individuals and companies to be Game Changers in the way they do business. *Global Cause Marketing* gives key insights encouraging businesses to be thought leaders and heroes by giving back in authentic and dynamic ways that connect with today's socially conscious consumers. Thank you Peter and Bob for your inspiration and helping change the course of history through your message.

-- Molly Bedingfield Founder and CEO, Global Angels Foundation and The Global Angel Awards

Peter & Bob have written a great book showing the tremendous impact a company can have on our communities, and grow their business at the same time. It's a win-win philosophy ... building your professional career by doing good! How can it get any better than that... the answer is it can't.

-- Michael King, Former CEO, KingWorld

Contents

First things First –
Mission is the new marketing!

A quick note to business owners: What follows in the pages ahead is the competitive advantage you have been searching for. Let's take a few things as assumptions. You already have a great product. Clearly, in today's competitive business environment, there is no substitute for excellence of product, executive leadership and staffing, as well as providing top-notch customer care. That's all the price of admission to the business ballpark. This book starts assuming those are in place. If they're not, put this book down and go back to the beginning. If they are, let's move forward. Consider this the new marketing of the 21ˢᵗ century. And here's the thing you need to know. It most likely won't cost you a penny more than you are already spending. You most likely allocate a portion of your budget toward charitable causes. That is important. Even admirable. Yet largely ineffective. Imagine, instead of random giving, what you could accomplish through targeted giving and channeling your budgeted charitable dollars to a specific program you design. Now you're in the game. And let's be clear: a targeted focused $100,000 can have significantly more powerful an impact than a random $1,000,000. So you don't need extra funds to enter the field of *Global Cause Marketing* and social entrepreneurship. You don't have to find new appropriation funds.

Think about your corporate image. We have been involved in countless meetings over the years where CEOs, marketing and advertising managers, brand managers or ad agency execs have been facing a huge challenge. They had to create a corporate image campaign. In the past companies would parade out a logo, or a slogan and build on those elements as an image. Over a period of corporate history, some companies relied on a product like a soft drink, or a smart phone, a household cleaner or a breakfast cereal to suffice as the corporation image. After all, Coca Cola is Coke, RIM is a little handheld device called a blackberry, Apple is an iPhone. As the iPhone is constantly battling the "latest and greatest" challengers (currently the Samsung Galaxy), as blackberry has been getting trashed by the tech media as a device not keeping up and as virtually all soft drinks continue to take a hit as an unhealthy sugar-water that gives drinkers diabetes and makes kids obese, public perception in these companies take a big plunge.

Media outlets looking for shock value immediately declare the impending death of these household names. Consumers jump on the bandwagon and start to Social Network bad news about the companies. And you have a corporate PR and image nightmare that will consume your every moment. Instead of spending your day moving your brands forward, you spend your time dealing with a mess. Welcome to the future of corporate image.

Brands can no longer hide behind the secured doors of your headquarters in the Midwest, Germany, Australia, or Silicon Valley. The Internet has blown your doors down and you're naked to the world. Every day people around the globe blog, twitter, and Facebook search your corporate soul. They know everything about you. Google is more powerful than any x-ray machine or body scanner. The collective population will know your story, good or bad quickly. So better make it good!

Every company wants to do the same thing. Build a good strong name, sell lots of goods or services and future-proof the company. Future-proofing your company means building a company name that allows you to immediately put a new product on the shelves and have people buy it because they trust the name. Nike has done their job well. They built the name with lots of great image ads, however very few actually focus on a specific shoe or product. While Nike has done it with big ad spending another shoe company has done it without the big media buys. Toms, the start up shoe company who basically took Argentinian workers soft shoes and put them on the feet of men and women in some of the most trendy and fashionable neighborhoods in America, selling them for $40 and up a pair. We hear this about Toms all the time: "I don't wear these shoes because they look beautiful or they are the best things for my feet. I wear them because I like what the company is about." Basically consumers feel good about the fact that they have a pair of Toms on their feet. Why? Because the shoes are a symbol of good social conscience and people are proud to display the symbol. Toms tiny ad campaign has been based on their corporate giving program- a pair of shoes to a kid who would otherwise not have shoes for every pair you buy. One for one.

The message is clear: people will support your company if they really know you're doing the right thing. That's what a successful corporate image is about for the future. And the world is watching and talking about you if you do the right thing. That's the best advertising you can hope for. But guess what. The world is also watching if you do the wrong thing. And that news spreads just as fast or faster.

Bob recently did a corporate image campaign for a major global brand client. He shot several commercials. One talked about the company, and the people in the company and the products. Another commercial spoke about a program the company has set up overseas helping people of a country doing sustainable farming. By far the most successful and well-liked commercial was the one about the farmers program. The message from consumers is clear. Consumers want to know that companies they support care and are about more than making a profit.

How many times have you watched CNN and seen corporate image commercials that all look generic. Many of these ads can just change the name of the company and basically the ad can be for almost any company. The images could come from a stock film library, kids splashing water, people at computers, the smiling faces, the dads, the moms, all the same basic scenes. Future generations will look at this and chuckle. It will have no positive effect whatsoever. You will waste your ad dollars.

We suggest a different approach. Take the money you are now investing in traditional advertising and add to it the money you are giving to charity. Combining the two expenditures can create an amazing future-proof corporate image for your company. The good news is you don't have to sacrifice anything you are now doing and even better news is that you don't have to go to the board of directors for more money. We want to be clear though. This is NOT a marketing gimmick, or simply an element of cause marketing. We ask you to search your company soul. Are you ready to have a global impact, and invest more than dollars? Are you ready to invest your heart?

The process works like this:

1. You start and maintain a program that demonstrates to the world your authentic company values;

2. You incorporate this message in to your present product advertising as specific corporate image campaigns;

3. The new programs provide you with something to talk about in new media and your website;

4. The money to fund this new program comes from a restructuring of your charitable donations. This will result in your charitable donations increasing and becoming sustainable.

You can achieve all of this without any additional corporate spending. And by the way, as you incorporate the T3 approach (investing your time, talent and treasure), you will see benefits such as happier and more productive employees and a legacy of good works. In short, your heart will change.

What is it that consumers really want to know about your company? They want to know what you are really doing for the world. Plain and simple. All the great speeches, funny or beautiful commercials, nice packaging and sales conventions are not going to cut it. You need a real message, one that's unique to your brand. People will support those brands that really do something for the world, not just for Wall Street and their stockholders.

This is the future of marketing, so embrace it and create a sustainable image, brand and company. The world is heading in this direction.

CAN A CAUSE MARKETING PROGRAM DO MORE HARM THAN GOOD?

Before we get into the heart and substance of this book, we have a question and a warning: Can a cause marketing program do more harm than good for your company? You bet it can. Create the wrong program and it will hurt your image. Hard as it is believe, donating money to charity can actually create a negative reaction from your customers.

Recently we went into the local "health-food" grocery store, which is part of a major international chain. Immediately before paying, the cashier said, "Do you want to contribute $1, $5, $20 or another amount to our foundation?" There is so much wrong with this approach that it is hard to begin. First, we didn't then and don't now have a clue as to what that foundation did, does or will do. Second, the cashiers ask that question to every consumer, no matter how many times he or she frequents that store in any given week or even day, de-valuing the relationship and making costumers feel embarrassed, ashamed, less-than and wanting to avoid the store. Third, when asked what the foundation does, the cashier didn't have any idea. In other words, neither the company employees nor the consumers had a clue what the contributions would support. There was an obvious breakdown in the communication of whatever the vision was supposed to be. And if it's unclear in the boardroom it'll be a fog in the aisles.

This, by the way, is happening at stores all across the country. Our experience happened to be at one of the most famous, high-priced, healthy supermarkets. We were paying top-dollar. We discussed this with a number of our friends who shop there and each one had a story as to how annoying the program was. A few actually said they no longer shop there because they don't want to feel guilty when buying groceries. And these words are from very generous people, radical givers.

Simply put, the above example is essentially a continuation of the old begging model. Sure, it's trendy to do a cause marketing program. Most companies are doing something, but they are not getting it right; they are hurting, rather than helping or building, their corporate image.

In just a single day, we experimented, going to a dog-groomer / pet-supply store, a pharmacy, and a traditional supermarket. At each, the question at the end of the purchase was, "Do you want to round up the change to the next highest dollar amount? We give that to charity." Here we go again. More stores asking for more money without stating a clear purpose; without adding any additional value, but adding heaps of guilt. At one store, we actually asked, "How about rounding down and giving us the change to give how we want?"

Bottom line: a well thought-out cause marketing initiative must be carefully planned. They must be tested like any other marketing plan. They must be organized from start to finish and established in a way so consumers will rally behind it. It's got to be heart-driven, communicated well throughout all levels of the organization, and it must inspire the consumers to feel good about supporting you and your brand. Be very clear about this: consumers want to feel that your company is adding value, not just asking them to pay more or give for an undefined cause. This is why the Toms Shoes project works so well. Toms is very clear that they are giving a pair of shoes to someone who doesn't have shoes. Toms doesn't ask you to donate money to buy a pair of shoes for a child. Of course, by purchasing a pair, we empower Toms to fulfill their purpose. But that's what a well thought-out cause marketing enterprise does. Your program must make the consumer feel good about buying from you. The structure and presentation of your cause marketing program is crucial. The very same program improperly presented will have a detrimental effect while the well-presented, carefully structured plan will hit a grand slam.

As it becomes more and more trendy to add a cause project, we have seen so many companies and boards of directors scramble to jump on board and create what they think are positive cause marketing programs. Usually, they have no background, experience or training in this specialized marketing. Companies that do only traditional marketing lack the expertise to create and structure a strong cause marketing plan. On the other side, companies that do only charity programs lack the experience to construct an effective cause marketing approach.

You don't want your customers walking away from the cashier complaining to his or her friends that they are being pressured or even hustled for even more money. That's detrimental cause marketing, and there's no need for this. Cause marketing can be incredibly effective, but it is essential that the plan be formed, organized and constructed by professional teams experienced in this unique brand of marketing.

Foreword

Generosity is a virtue in corporations as well as individuals. We respect firms that give consistently to the needy of our community and support public institutions such as universities, museums, zoos, and symphony orchestras. Marketing studies show again and again that we prefer to do business with such companies.

But the American business climate is undergoing a radical shift. Increasingly, we expect corporations to be more than generous benefactors; we expect them to *be involved* in alleviating the needs of our world. We expect executives and top employees to invest more than their company's money in causes we support; to put it bluntly, *we expect them to invest themselves* in the effort to change other people's lives.

The public still believes philanthropic giving is important—more than ever, since cash-starved governments must cut their funding of humanitarian efforts—but the proxy power of money, which gives it so much flexibility in everyday commerce, makes it inadequate to fill human need. Money is too impersonal for that. When people are hungry or homeless, shoeless or shirtless, oppressed or outcast by society, their needs cannot be filled by money alone or even the things money can buy.

They need personal contact from other human beings who care about their needs.

For this reason, the twenty-first century is giving birth to a new economic model which we call *Global Cause Marketing*. Unlike the philanthropic capitalism of the nineteenth century or sponsorship capitalism of the twentieth century, *Global Cause Marketing* inspires its constituents to give their own *time, talent,* and *treasure* (T3) to lift the burdens of their neighbors.

This book explores how *Global Cause Marketing* is already changing the nature of human society. It explains how you can be part of this groundswell without the distraction of perpetual fund-raising projects. It provides dozens of case histories to prove that you can shift your philanthropic resources to build a sustainable business, whose day-to-day operations will grow a healthier, more equitable world.

Most important, *Global Cause Marketing* is about living a significant life. In the nineteenth and twentieth centuries, we idolized the self-made, successful businessperson. But the traditional perks of success no longer motivate many of us to get out of bed in the morning. We want to change people's lives for the better.

We have learned that success is what happens to us, but significance is what happens through us. With the right luck and pluck, anyone can be successful. But only compassionate, servant-hearted people will be significant when the story of our generation is told—and we want to be among them.

So if you are looking for a hot stock tip or smart tax strategy, you'd better look elsewhere. But if you want to make our world a better place to live, read on.

1. Game Changer

"The purpose of business is to create and keep a customer." That dictum of business, says guru Peter F. Drucker guided America's leading corporations for a generation. Marketing execs focused on selecting the most profitable customers, learning their wants and needs, and testing various sales appeals to find one that hit their customers' "sweet spot." If an astute marketing team could do that year after year, their company was sure to outscore its rivals.

But the rules have changed. In fact, the whole game has changed.

Imagine challenging your company's chief rival to a beach volleyball tournament. You both have skillful teams, high-energy players, and a relentless competitive spirit. And it's a perfect afternoon at the beach—pleasant, sunny skies with sea gulls wheeling overhead and the relaxing rhythm of waves washing up on sugar-white sand. Love-struck couples walk hand-in-hand, sunbathers laze on their blankets, children laugh as they raise a sand castle nearby.

So the match begins. Your team does well. You keep widening your lead on your opponents' score as you volley the ball with ease and grace, like a well-choreographed dance troupe.

The match point comes after a particularly long volley, from one teammate to another, until the ball comes to you. With a high jump and a pivot, you use both hands to drive it over your back in a power spike that your opponents can't possibly return. It's your best play ever.

But your teammates are not celebrating. They're not even smiling. In fact, their faces are a strange mixture of puzzlement, dismay, and terror. So you whip around to see what happened to the ball.

The other team has disappeared, along with the castle-builders, sunbathers, and starry-eyed romantics. The beach is vacant and eerily quiet. No children laughing. No birds squawking. Not even the calm rhythm of ocean surf. Your eyes follow the ball, rolling down the wet sand, and you realize that the tide has suddenly dropped. Your net-mate gasps and points frantically out to sea. With a pang of fear, you see a massive wall of water five stories high, racing toward your idyllic little beach. It's a tsunami. Nobody cares who won the last volley, because the game has changed—and your rivals have taken the high ground.

This is the business environment of twenty-first-century America. Creating customers is no longer your priority; creating a better life for them is.

A Good Product Isn't Good Enough

Ask executives at Nestlé, the multinational conglomerate that American consumers trust for healthy products such as bottled water, chocolate milk, and infant formula. In the mid-1970's, an exposé revealed that Nestlé's marketing of infant formula had lethal consequences. Mothers in India and Africa took Nestlé's upbeat advertising to heart. They started giving babies the formula instead of breast milk and, to stretch their meager resources, they diluted the formula. Thousands of children died of malnutrition.

The World Health Organization and UNICEF reprimanded Nestlé and consumer groups boycotted their products. For making a defective product? No. For false advertising? No. For improper labeling? No. For failing to come alongside their customers to make sure they used its products properly.

Ironically, Nestlé donates millions to charities every year to curry public goodwill, while it keeps on selling infant formula in the Third World without teaching mothers how to use it. So the boycott continues. In fact, a leading breast-cancer charity in England turned down a Nestlé donation of £1 million because of the infant formula scandal. That's what we call marketing malpractice. When companies think only of finding new customers for their products, they are sure to be guilty of it.

About the time Nestle got the first salvo of media criticism for its infant formula promotions, other corporations began waking up to the fact that the marketing game had changed. Bruce W. Burtch, marketing strategist for a major foundation based in San Francisco, told his director that their objective should be to "do well by doing good." In other words, they would attract plenty of financial support if they were involved in the everyday lives of their people they served. They were not in the business of raising and disbursing money, but rather the business of bettering people's lives. The objective of the old marketing game was, "Make the most money by making and retaining the most customers." Yet Burtch's 1976 phrase became the objective of a new wave of corporate social responsibility: *Do well by doing good.*

Heightened Social Awareness

In retrospect, the change was inevitable. We live in an era of heightened social awareness because communications technology makes news of human need so immediate and so widely available. When a magnitude 7.0 earthquake convulsed the island nation of Haiti in January 2010, thousands of photos and videos went out via Twitter and Facebook. When a stronger earthquake struck Japan in March 2011, cell-phone tweets (more than *1,200 per minute* in Tokyo alone) alerted seaside residents to flee from the impending tsunami before government emergency bulletins could be broadcast. Our global "village" is so well wired that we know instantly when distant peoples need our help.

(Have you wondered why you see fewer appeals for disaster relief and food aid on late-night TV? It's because you now get the information in "real time" on your cell phone and laptop computer.)

This heightened social awareness makes our employees and customers want to do more than write a check in response to people's needs. They want to change their global neighbors' lives for the better. So traditional corporate charity appeals ("For every burger you buy, we'll donate fifty cents to this cause...") fall on deaf ears. People want to patronize companies that are on the ground in needy regions of the world, making a sustainable difference in local residents' quality of life. Our best and brightest young people want to work for those companies, too.

This heightened social awareness draws us to companies that treat people with equality and integrity. Facebook "likes" can build a loyal following for a company that the public feels is excelling in these areas. On the other hand, boycotts can "go viral" within an hour, due to Facebook posts and cellular "tweets."

Remember the July 2012 brouhaha when a son of the founder of Chick-fil-A told a Baptist newspaper that the company supported "the biblical definition of the family unit"? Investigative reporters found that the restaurant chain's charitable foundation supported groups lobbying against same-sex marriage. A nationwide boycott of Chick-fil-A followed, with a nationwide "Support Chick-fil-A Wednesday" quick on its heels — both orchestrated with electronic social media. In a desperate effort at damage control, the company issued a press release that said:

The Chick-fil-A culture and service tradition in our restaurants is to treat every person with honor, dignity and respect–regardless of their belief, race, creed, sexual orientation or gender. We will continue this tradition in the over 1,600 restaurants run by independent Owner/Operators. Going forward, our intent is to leave the policy debate over same-sex marriage to the government and political arena.[1]

Not exactly the kind of back-pedaling that any corporate PR department wants to do!

Techno-enhanced social awareness makes it easier to reward companies that use the earth's resources responsibly. One blogger writes:

I've always been a tap drinker — it's refreshing, healthy, and free — but when some genius started putting H2O in plastic containers and selling it for a dollar a pop, Americans went nuts. Water? In a bottle?! As popular as it became, you'd think they were filled at the Fountain of Youth...

The problem is, we're just too lazy to turn on our sinks and fill up a reusable bottle. Because if we did that, it might mean we have to wash it every now and then — and, well, that's just not worth the effort, right?

With this post, I hope to change that attitude. I've chosen seven reusable, affordable, eco-friendly (all BPA-free) bottles to rate. Because they each have different features, I've established four categories on which to judge the bottles — style, design, price, and versatility. Which bottle is best for you? Find out below.[2]

He gives glowing testimonials for seven styles of ecologically friendly, disposable water bottles, complete with photos, prices, and links to retail websites where they can be purchased. (Talk about free advertising!) He then offers followers the option to comment on this post or "like" it on their own Facebook, Twitter, or LinkedIn accounts-and several have done just that.

Electronic social media accelerate the pace of public comment and response to corporate behavior. Executives who ignore this fact do so at their peril.

Conversely, social entrepreneurs use the same communications technology to enable constituents to "do good" all the time, not just in their spare time. They create and host electronic bulletin boards, blogs, and discussion groups where thousands of like-minded people can share their passion for a cause and organize their involvement in it. Organizations doing this earn the respect and loyalty of their employees and customers-as well as their patronage and the profits that come with it!

Yes, the game of corporate marketing has changed. The objective is now to promote social entrepreneurship, the business of "doing well by doing good." That's the formula for corporate success in the twenty-first century.

2. Who Says It's Not Profitable?

ritics have good reasons to be skeptical about the profitability of social entrepreneurship. Virtually every national company has jumped on the bandwagon, producing an annual report to prove its engagement in the social needs of its constituents. These corporate social responsibility (CSR) reports use every imaginable standard to suggest that a company is on the cutting edge of the new movement. Their fuzzy metrics drive business journalists back to the traditional dollar-and-sense standard of profit, but there's another problem: Methods of accounting for sustainability and systemic social benefit are at such an early stage of evolution that it's difficult to know how much of a company's profits to attribute to these activities. As a result an exhaustive study published in the March 2012 issue of the *Journal of Economic Literature* had to conclude there was "no strong positive or negative link between social responsibility and financial performance."[3]

Critics are skeptical of social entrepreneurs' profit reports because business owners have long used philanthropy to maintain a façade of success. That's why a couple of fellows expected to collect a nice donation for poor relief on Christmas Eve 1843, when they called at the London firm of Scrooge & Marley.

"A few of us are endeavoring to raise a fund to buy the poor some meat and drink and means of warmth," one of them said. "...What shall I put you down for?"

"Nothing!" Scrooge replied.

"You wish to be anonymous?"

"I wish to be left alone," Scrooge replied. "...I help to support the establishments I have mentioned [prisons, work houses, governmental assistance]. They cost enough, and those who are badly off must go there."

The fund raiser urged him to learn more about the plight of homeless people in his city, but Scrooge scowled, "It's not my business. It's enough for a man to understand his own business, and not to interfere with other people's. Mine occupies me constantly. Good afternoon, gentlemen!"

We may fault Scrooge for his stinginess, but not for his business acumen. He knew that generous charitable donations don't prove that a company's making money.

Snapshots of Significance

For a company to turn a profit while feeding hungry people, putting shoes on school children, or cleaning up toxic waste seems...well, a little too good to be true. But we'll introduce you to dozens of profitable social entrepreneurs in this book. Let's start with a few snapshots:

Paul Hawken started his professional life as a press photographer covering the civil rights movement of the 1960's. He developed a passion for making a difference in this world, so he began launching a series of businesses dedicated to environmental preservation and good health. They prospered to such an extent that he wrote a best-selling book entitled, *Growing a Business,* and the Public Broadcasting System invited him to host a 17-part television series based on it. In 2002, *Fortune* magazine observed, "Today Hawken occupies a unique niche in the American landscape, combining bottom-line business credentials with credibility among environmentalists and social critics…[He believes] that business—with its restless energy, imagination, and creativity—will one day get us out of the mess it has made."[4]

When *George Siemon* announced a meeting of family farmers at a Wisconsin county courthouse in 1988, the outlook was bleak. Family farms were folding, government subsidies were falling, and not many people were willing to pay a premium for the organic produce that George and his friends had to sell. But seven of them signed on to the idea of forming an organic farmers' cooperative, which they called the Coulee Region Organic Produce Pool (CROPP). Organic farmers coast-to-coast have since joined the organization, which now has nearly eighteen hundred members. Their sales topped $715 million in 2011 with profits of $13.3 million. "We are committed to organic agriculture and building a future for sustainable family farming in America," a CROPP spokesman says.[5]

Brent Freeman was a young commodities trader who crafted an incredibly profitable deal with two of his friends in 2009, and they wound up with enough money to start their own brokerage in Asia. Instead, they chose to start a web site called Rooszt. com, which markets the products of companies committed to "global humanitarian, eco-friendly, ethical or community-support." In a recent interview with *Fast Company*, Brent cracked that their shoppers "get real 'change' for their dollar."[6] They have plenty of potential clients, too. B Lab, a nonprofit organization that certifies these cause-oriented brands, reported in 2009 that more than thirty thousand of them can be found in the American marketplace with combined annual sales of more than $40 billion.[7]

Socially Responsible Investing

Investors see the profit potential of social entrepreneurs, because venture capital is flowing into these enterprises at a quickening pace. Acumen Capital was one of the first, and it has now invested $69 million in social entrepreneurial firms in India, Pakistan, and Africa. Banker Jacqueline Novogratz began Acumen in the wake of 9/11, when she convened a conference of foreign-policy experts to discuss the cause of these terrorist attacks. A member of the audience asked what she would do about terrorism if someone gave her a million dollars. She said she would go to the terrorists' home countries to establish institutions that would give their people "a sense of hope and possibility." Within weeks, two anonymous gifts totaling a million dollars arrived at her office, so Novogratz went to Pakistan. The fund has subsequently invested $13 million there.

Of the 65 companies that have received Acumen loans in the past decade, 11 have repaid them in full and 10 are profitable. Only 3 of the companies have failed, compared to a 50-percent failure rate for typical venture capital recipients.[8] Other venture capital firms report similar success rates from social entrepreneurs. Consultant Olivia Khalili offers this explanation: "Having a social mission is not a drain on company assets or a tangential program, it is a business strategy that yields a competitive advantage, which smaller companies can better leverage."[9]

Brokerage firms also know a good thing when they see it and have begun to package the stocks of socially responsible companies as mutual funds. Take Walden Social Equity Fund (WSEFX), for example. *Money* Magazine notes, "This fund takes a nuanced approach to socially responsible investing...It evaluates companies' corporate governance, environmental impacts, community relations, and workplace conditions, among other factors." The result? "The fund has certainly had some off years, but its long-term performance is hard to argue with: Its trailing 10-year returns put it in the top 5 percent of Morningstar's large-growth category."[10] Other funds of socially responsible companies have produced attractive returns. The Forum for Sustainable and Responsible Investment notes the growing importance of this investment strategy:

Sustainable and Responsible Investing (SRI) is a broad-based approach to investing that now encompasses an estimated $3.07 trillion out of $25.2 trillion in the U.S. investment marketplace today. SRI recognizes that corporate responsibility and societal concerns are valid parts of investment decisions. SRI considers both the investor's financial needs and an investment's impact on society. SRI investors encourage corporations to improve their practices on environmental, social, and governance issues. You may also hear SRI-like approaches to investing referred to as mission investing, responsible investing, double or triple bottom line investing, ethical investing, sustainable investing, or green investing.

As a result of its investing strategies, SRI also works to enhance the bottom lines of the companies in question and, in so doing, delivers more long-term wealth to shareholders. In addition, SRI investors seek to build wealth in underserved communities worldwide. With SRI, investors can put their money to work to build a more sustainable world while earning competitive returns both today and over time.[11]

The keen interest of investors, investment brokers, and venture capital firms confirms the profit potential of social entrepreneurship. This is not just doing "business with a heart," but doing business with a clear-eyed focus on the bottom line.

3. Marketing Malpractice

The rapid growth of social entrepreneurship may lead you to think that your most prudent strategy is to sit on the sidelines until the rules of the game are well-established. Why get involved in any social cause if you can just mind your own knitting? Why try to become an engine of global change if you can just announce a corporate sponsorship here and there? Why not leave "that cause marketing thing" to a few wild-eyed fanatics — you know, the Occupy Wall Street crowd — so you can focus on gross margins and economies of scale?

Here's why: Companies that *don't* become social entrepreneurs are being found guilty of marketing malpractice. That charge has been leveled against some of the most consumer-friendly companies in America, "household names" that we seldom associate with corporate malfeasance. Yet consumers, stockholders, and now even the civil courts are taking these accusations seriously. You should, too.

What Is Malpractice?

Marketing consultant Aaron Douglass[12] identifies three types of corporate behavior that may be considered marketing malpractice: negligence, lack of due diligence, and loss of chance.

Negligence – When a company fails to do what competent professionals in its field would do to protect individuals from foreseeable harm. "Negligence is not the same as carelessness," Douglass notes, "because someone might be exercising as much care as possible, but still fall short of the competence expected of them."

For example, suppose your company provides agricultural irrigation services. You are scrupulous to avoid infringing on the water rights of your customers' neighbors. You install state-of-the-art filters at your pumping stations to protect native fish populations. You artfully conceal your equipment to avoid ruining the aesthetics of the countryside. But as you sign up new clients, you don't mention that some farmers who use your services eventually see their crop yields *collapse* because river water increases the salinity of their soil. You figure that's not your concern, so long as you provide the services they want. But if you fail to protect them from foreseeable harm that could be caused by your services, you're being negligent. And that's malpractice.

Lack of Due Diligence – Douglass notes that we normally think of due diligence as "performance of an investigation of a business or person prior to signing of a contract or entering a relationship." You would be careful to investigate the background of another company you wanted to acquire, for example. But what about the customers you seek to acquire? How much do you know about their way of life, their weaknesses and vulnerabilities, and the impact your business will have upon them?

Suppose you operate a cluster of grain elevators and you get a lucrative contract from an organic farmers' co-op. You agree to load their wheat crop on a freighter that plies the Great Lakes; however, the co-op's elevator is a few hundred bushels short. No problem — you have others — so you top off the load with grain from another elevator. A couple of weeks later, a government official from Quebec shows up, clipboard in hand, and begins asking questions. When she learns that you topped off the co-op's shipment with grain from another source, she ends the interview. It turns out that Quebec has extremely high standards for advertising a product as "organic," and your good intentions has cost the farmers' co-op their biggest account in Canada. You failed to use due diligence in getting to know your customers and their customers. That's malpractice.

Loss of Chance – A third common offense of marketing malpractice is what Douglass calls "loss of chance." Briefly described, "Loss of chance is an issue of causation where the negligence of a professional deprives a client of the opportunity to obtain a benefit or avoid a loss."

Now you're the owner of a sugar-cane plantation in Florida. Business is brisk, but every year you must explain to your stockholders how you are dealing with a persistent problem: what to do with several hundred tons of cane pulp that come out of your sugar refinery every day. Your first solution was to hire a disposal company to haul it out into the Atlantic and dump it every couple of weeks; but city officials at Cocoa Beach were not too happy when your refuse started washing ashore. You built a massive incinerator to burn the stuff, but couldn't get your emissions into acceptable environmental limits. An on-site landfill is your current solution, but neighbors complain about the noise of your dump trucks and bulldozers running around the clock. In the midst of a contentious stockholders' meeting, a soft-spoken retiree asks why you don't do as your competitors in South America, who turn the cane pulp into paper. Silence. You learn in a subsequent court hearing that your stockholders have lost millions in paper revenue — not to mention hundreds of thousands in disposal fees and litigation — so they are suing you for malpractice.

How to Mitigate Risk

So how do you mitigate the risk of marketing malpractice? Is it a matter of following government regulations? Certainly, that's critical. Today's business executive faces a thicket of environmental and health regulations, as illustrated by a recent string of lawsuits won by the City of San Diego, California[13]:

- San Diego and several other California municipalities sued the Target Corporation for the improper storage and disposal of hazardous wastes such as discarded tires and defective aerosol cans. Target was found guilty in March 2011 and ordered to pay $22.5 million.

- San Diego and 44 other cities sued CVS Pharmacies for the improper storage and disposal of hazardous waste, including outdated over-the-counter medicines and household cleaning solvents. CVS was found guilty in April 2012 and ordered to pay $11.75 million.

- San Diego sued San Diego Gas & Electric for losses stemming from two 2007 wildfires sparked by the utility's power lines, among other things. SDG&E settled out of court in June 2012 for $27 million.

Environmental laws are so stringent in some states that a reputable company may find itself on the losing end of a lawsuit for *appearing* to violate them.

"No good deed goes unpunished," cynics would say, yet no one can deny that good environmental laws are necessary. Laws governing how we label and promote our services help to inform everyone about the environmental impact of decisions we make. When the Federal Trade Commission updated its guidelines for environmentally-friendly labeling in September 2012, FTC Chairman Jon Leibowitz said, "Most marketers are honest. They are not in the business of lying to consumers. But what we need is a little more clarity."14

So the new guidelines require companies to do a careful trade-off analysis before they advertise a product as being "green" or "environmentally friendly." For example, you can no longer label your product as being "green" just because you use a certain percentage of recycled content, if transporting the scrap material and recovering that content damages the environment more than you would have done by using raw materials. Christopher A. Cole, partner in the marketing practice of law firm Manatt, Phelps & Phillips, cautions marketing professionals to study the FTC's 314-page *Green Guides* with care. "These are not laws, but they are guidance," he explained. "You ignore them at your peril."15

The FTC enforces Federal truth-in-advertising laws, so its *Green Guides* do have legal teeth. However, plenty of individuals and private organizations act as watchdogs in the environmental arena, and they are ready to blow the whistle on firms they believe are making overblown environmental claims. Law firm Ice Miller LLP reports that "lawsuits and class actions accusing companies of "greenwashing"- marketing the environmental friendliness of a company's product in a false or misleading way-have sprung up across the nation. These lawsuits have been filed against companies in a variety of industries and trades, including construction companies, retailers, automakers, candy makers and manufacturers of cleaning supplies."

Ice Miller advises, "Although green marketing is a potentially invaluable tool, companies should ensure that they understand and minimize the risks that are associated with its use."16

EnviroMedia Social Marketing, a firm that specializes in marketing the environmental efforts of socially responsible companies, has partnered with the University of Oregon School of Journalism and Communications to rate "green" claims on a "Greenwashing Index" (http://www.greenwashingindex.com). They offer these illustrations:

A classic example is an energy company that runs an advertising campaign touting a "green" technology they're working on — but that "green" technology represents only a sliver of the company's otherwise not-so-green business, or may be marketed on the heels of an oil spill or plant explosion.

Or a hotel chain that calls itself "green" because it allows guests to choose to sleep on the same sheets and reuse towels, but actually does very little to save water and energy where it counts — on its grounds, with its appliances and lighting, in its kitchens, and with its vehicle fleet.

Or a bank that's suddenly "green" because you can conduct your finances online, or a grocery store that's "green" because they'll take back your plastic grocery bags, or …

You get the picture.[17]

The Greenwashing Index invites the public to rate the environmental claims of product labels, commercials, even public-service announcements on a scale from 1 ("Authentic") to 5 ("Bogus"), and an advisory panel screens the ratings before they are posted. You may want to check whether your own company's messages are rated on the index. The same alliance has just launched another site called the "Leanwashing Index" to rate health claims of various products from fast food to exercise equipment and footwear (http://www.leanwashing.com).

Your Professional Duty

However, marketing malpractice involves more than running afoul of the law or public opinion; it's an overall failure to fulfill your professional duty to stockholders, customers, and your community. The *Harvard Business Review* noted nearly a decade ago that many good companies are in a "death spiral of serial product failure, missed opportunity, and squandered wealth" because they ignore customers' real needs and the impact that their businesses have on communities where they operate.[18] Don't let your company become one of them.

As *Global Cause Marketing* takes center stage, your company should be in the spotlight. A business feature in *Time* recently discussed, "Why Companies Can No Longer Afford to Ignore Their Social Responsibilities," quoting Wharton's Professor Eric Orts who said that corporate social responsibility "has to be integrated into the DNA of the enterprise. Companies need to say: 'We want to make money, sure, but we also care about our effect on society and the environment. And that comes through in the kinds of jobs we provide, the kinds of products we make and the ways in which we use resources.'"[19]

Sensitive to stockholder concerns about these issues, many companies now circulate an annual corporate social responsibility (CSR) report.[20] Here's how Nike CEO Mark Parker introduced his company's 2010 CSR: "This report is published at a tipping point. It's time for the world to shift."[21] The 176-page presentation then reviewed Nike's commitment to sustainable manufacturing, minimal environmental impacts, and improved labor conditions in its third-world factories.

Accounting giant Deloitte finds at least six thousand "organizations around the globe investing significant time and effort in monitoring and disclosing their sustainability performance, or ESG — environmental, social and governance — performance, usually in a sustainability report that is separate from a financial statement."[22]

Seven states have taken this a step farther, establishing a legal class of incorporation for companies that provide certain social benefits to their communities. (In Georgia, it's known as the Benefit Corporation or "B Corp.") If a company proves each year that it delivers these benefits to people of the state, its investors receive some generous tax breaks. Matthew May, CPA for an Atlanta accounting firm that caters to B Corp start-ups, offers this assessment of the trend:

> Benefit Corps are going to attract a distinct kind of investor to a new start-up. Much like mutual funds that focus on investing in companies that meet specific social or ethical guidelines are gaining traction, Benefit Corps are a similar vehicle for a start-up…
>
> Definitely, I think that investors could target specific B Corps whose mission and values align with theirs. This downturn has caused many to re-evaluate everything about their financial lives, and where to invest money should be at the top of that list.[23]

Investors who *don't* put their money into social entrepreneurs expose their capital to increased risk due to the threat of litigation, lack of business sustainability, and competitive disadvantage. Let's consider each of these briefly.

Risk of Litigation. Our previous examples of environmental litigation should be convincing. Think you might escape this risk by going offshore? Then consider a couple of recent news stories about American enterprises slapped with heavy fines for their misdeeds overseas:

- Buenos Aires (Nov. 8, 2012) -- An Argentine judge froze Chevron's assets in the country Wednesday at the request of a court in Ecuador, where the US oil giant has been ordered to pay $19 billion for environmental damage, plaintiffs said. Enrique Bruchou, an attorney for the plaintiffs here, noted that Chevron only holds $2 billion in assets in Argentina....

  In October, Chevron said it was disappointed by the US Supreme Court's decision not to block the massive fine sought by Ecuador for environmental damage in the Amazon…The Ecuadoran complaint stems from years of unchecked pollution in the Amazon attributed to Texaco Petroleum, which Chevron acquired in 2001.

Texaco polluted large areas of Ecuador's Amazon jungle when it operated in the region from 1964 to 1990, a decade before being acquired by Chevron, according to indigenous groups and local farmers.[24]

- Washington, D.C. (Aug. 20, 2012) - Karen Sack, director of international ocean conservation for the Pew Environment Group, issued the following statement in response to a major decision…The U.S. District Court for the Southern District of New York ordered three defendants to pay $54.9 million in restitution to the South African government for illegally taking lobsters from the country's waters over a five-year period. "Pew applauds the court for recognizing the severity of this crime and appropriately ordering such a high penalty.

"These defendants stole an environmental asset from South Africa, and it is only fair that they pay the country back for that theft. This unprecedented ruling shows that the U.S. can and will take concerted action to stop illegal fishing and bring those U.S. citizens engaging in it to justice, whether it has occurred within or outside of U.S. waters. Most of the illegal catch was shipped to the United States for sale. This is the largest ever restitution awarded by a U.S. court under the historic Lacey Act, one of the oldest American conservation laws that…prohibits trade in wildlife, fish, and plants that have been illegally taken, transported, or sold."[25]

Imagine such ruinous penalties being levied against an enterprise where you have invested a substantial sum. Malpractice does not come cheap, especially in the realm of corporate social responsibility.

Will This Business Survive?

Lack of business sustainability. What steps should a company take to assure that its operations are sustainable? In a later chapter, we will consider how a corporation can safeguard the environmental and social sustainability of communities where it does business; but first we need to raise a more fundamental question: Is your business economically viable? Will changes in market demand, the availability of raw materials, or other factors doom your future if you continue on your present course? These are questions that every conscientious investor and corporate executive must answer.

What would you say is the sustainability outlook of the property and casualty insurance business? Several years of hurricanes, floods, tornadoes, and other natural disasters have required insurers to pay out record settlements. Industry veterans argue that's just the nature of the business: Premiums paid in mild-weather years offset the losses of severe-weather years. But what if the weather cycles are getting out of whack, due to global climate change? Is the traditional business model sustainable?

Citing its "substantially weakened financial position" in 2009, State Farm Florida submitted a two-year plan to exit the homeowners' insurance business in that state. The insurance commissioner allowed the company to stop writing new policies, but not to drop existing ones-and there has been a running battle over rate increases ever since. In the fall of 2012, State Farm Florida asked permission to raise homeowners' rates an average 14.9 percent, but the rate commission approved an average increase of 6.4 percent.

State Farm Florida "had seen its surplus drop from $822 million in 2007 to $368 million in 2011," the *Insurance Journal* reports. "They also said that following the 2004 hurricane season it had to borrow $750 million from its parent company, State Farm Mutual, an amount it has yet to pay back."[26]

Three states (New York, Washington, and California) now require insurers to submit an annual report of their plans to deal with climate change. "Global warming presents unique risks, and it is vital that our insurance industry adequately account for the impacts of climate change," says Benjamin M. Lawsky, superintendent of New York's civil-service pension fund. "We look forward to working with the industry to address these important and growing risks."

A lot of work remains to be done. Only 11 of the 88 insurers that reported to New York last year had any written plan to deal with the costs of climate change.[27] "…There is a high level of concern among insurers about the impacts of climate change that is not matched by concrete plans to deal with those impacts," observes Andrew Logan, director of Ceres, a nonprofit coalition that vets these reports. "There is a real gap between the risk that's been identified and plans to address it."[28]

Have you placed your retirement funds in the hands of an insurance company that cannot cope with a string of 100-year floods? Investors have to think about business sustainability.

Taking the Moral High Ground

Competitive Disadvantage. For the past two centuries, business owners knew they could gain a competitive edge with proprietary products, cheaper production, or more efficient distribution, but the rules of competition are changing. In the twenty-first century, companies that let their competitors take the "moral high ground" lose market share. The Cause Marketing Forum has a growing mountain of evidence to substantiate this[29]:

- *2008:* The annual Cone Cause Evolution Study sponsored by Duke University showed that when Americans have a choice between two competing brands of similar quality and price, 79% will switch to the brand associated with a cause they support (compared to 66% in a similar 1993 study).

- *2009:* The annual BBMG Conscious Consumer® Report found that 72% of the Americans say they avoid buying from companies whose practices they disagree with.

- *2010:* The annual Edelman Goodpurpose® study found that 86% of respondents worldwide expect corporations to devote as much attention to societal concerns as they do to business concerns.
- *2011:* The annual Cone Cause Evolution Study found that 93% of consumers worldwide want to know what companies are doing to make the world a better place.

- *2012:* The annual Edelman Goodpurpose® study found that 47% of respondents worldwide had purchased a specific product to support a societal cause in the previous 12 months.

The competitive advantage of *Global Cause Marketing* is most obvious in emerging markets, where consumers know that a company's efforts to improve working conditions, clean up the environment, and safeguard community health will have a direct impact on them. Former Communist countries of Eastern Europe provide a fascinating case study in this regard, since management experts have advised petroleum companies there to divert money from their environmental public-relations efforts to actually clean up their act. Here's the advice that two professors at the Polytechnic University of Bucharest gave graduate management students in 2006:

> Today,...many billions of dollars are spent every
> year on philanthropy and CSR initiatives. Billions
> more are spent on the defensive advertising, lobbying,
> and PR with which companies attempt to shirk from
> the social concerns for which they are blamed. These
> resources, already committed, could be spent far more
> effectively without detracting from the company's
> overall purpose. Companies that choose the new
> path will reap disproportionate rewards by build-
> ing sustainable reputations that far outdistance their
> competitors...[30]

We wish we could report that their students took the advice
to heart. Romania's refiners managed to reach minimum com-
pliance with environmental laws so that country could enter the
European Union in 2007, but they have made no genuine commitment to changing their business since then. The *Petroleum
Industry Review* lamented in June 2012 that Romanians are likely
to get most of their oil from Western refineries in the future.
Romania's "still-underinvested and not yet upgraded refining
technology landscape are hindering integration with the local
market and are favoring fuels [import] instead...The market
gives no one a free ride..."[31]

Certainly not.

4. *Global Cause Marketing* Defined

B efore we go farther in exploring this new form of business, we need to gain a clear understanding of what it is. Business commentators apply a variety of terms to this phenomenon, including:

- Cause Marketing
- Green initiative
- Mission enterprise
- Social entrepreneurship
- Socially responsible business
- Sustainable business
- Triple-bottom-line business

We should set aside a couple of myths, however. First, we are not simply talking about corporate philanthropy. Important social causes have always needed generous, sustaining financial contributions from the corporate world. How many public-broadcasting stations, fine-arts centers, universities, hospitals, and zoos would have disappeared without a torrent of philanthropic gifts, year after year? Black-tie dinners and charity balls have rescued many a public institution from bankruptcy.

Billionaires such as Warren Buffett and Bill Gates have raised public awareness of the need for philanthropic largesse. Both

men have pledged half of their substantial fortunes to philanthropic causes when they die-and challenged others to follow
suit. *The Huffington Post* reported in September 2012 that 92
wealthy individuals have signed their "Giving Pledge," including the likes of Facebook founder Mark Zuckerberg and New
York Mayor Michael Bloomberg.[32]

Philanthropists of past generations left their mark upon the
American landscape, such as the hundreds of public libraries established by steel magnate Andrew Carnegie, yet that pales in com-
parison to what's currently happening with philanthropic giving.
Economists say we are at the leading edge of the greatest transfer
for wealth from one generation to another in the history of the
Western world, as Baby Boomers die and leave their capital to their
children or to the causes they support. Corporate philanthropy will
be no less significant. It's a safe bet that philanthropic giving will
exert a formative influence upon Western culture for years to come.

But that's not what we're talking about.

Your Mission: To Change the World

Second, this new movement is not just a politically correct form
of public relations. Certainly, major corporations have learned
the importance of having savvy public relations people on their
team. When there's a major environmental accident such as the
BP's Deep Sea Horizon oil rig explosion or Union Carbide's
Bhopal pesticide plant gas leak, P.R. people spring into action
to inform and reassure the public. Preemptively, corporate public relations can build a favorable reputation in the public eye
by sponsoring community events that portray a company as a
responsible member of local society. When trouble comes (and
it surely will), such favorable positioning in public opinion will
help a beleaguered company to weather the storm.

So many corporate P.R. specialists stake out positions for
their clients in causes that are supported by large segments
of their constituency-Breast Cancer Awareness, the Muscular

Dystrophy Marathon, Adopt-A-Highway, and others. These "politically correct" P.R. positions are not likely to draw criticism, but endear corporate sponsors to their customers. Nothing wrong with that. And it's surely a more constructive way to spend a company's promotional budget than on cuddly bunnies and snappy radio jingles.

But politically correct P.R. is not what we are talking about, either.

Social entrepreneurship is using entrepreneurial skill and for-profit principles to solve global, social issues. Social entrepreneurs don't simply add a social cause to their company's advertising campaigns; they don't simply allocate a percentage of their annual budget for public causes as a gesture of goodwill. They commit their businesses to the task of changing the world for the better. Their corporate purpose is social transformation. And they are able to do it profitably, so they can sustain and expand their influence upon society.

Social entrepreneurs combine creativity, the principles of entrepreneurship, and a personal hunger to solve a social issue. Call them "activists" if you will (or "subversives," if you feel threatened by them), you cannot deny that they are a force to be reckoned with.

David Elliott, the CEO of a high-tech semiconductor company in Silicon Valley, felt there ought to be a way to use their ceramic technology to make an economical water filter for villages where people have no access to public sanitation or water treatment. In 2005, his team devised a simple way to make such a filter using readily available materials such as clay and sawdust. In Nepal, they partnered with a successful pottery entrepreneur to launch the first franchise of their system. He enlisted hundreds of local potters to make, distribute, and check the results of the five-dollar ceramic water filters. Now known as Village Forward, the nonprofit organization licenses its technology to for-profit entrepreneurs in villages throughout that Himalayan country. They describe their business model in a Manifesto which says:

Village Forward develops for-profit micro-franchises in Nepal that locally make and sell affordable water filters. Its mission is to provide safe water and economic opportunity through social business. Village Forward is a not-for-profit that stands for profit-making. 100% of micro-franchisees- profits are kept locally to reinvest in their families, businesses, and ultimately the health of their communities.[33]

Creativity, entrepreneurial spirit, and a passion to solve a critical social problem-these are vital characteristics of any social entrepreneur.

Notice Village Forward's emphasis on profitability. Social entrepreneurs make their efforts financially sustainable through operational revenue, rather than seeking donations or outside sponsorship. While Village Forward does accept donations on its website, here's how they picture the difference between traditional charity giving and investing in a for-profit social enterprise:

Source: http://www.villageforward.org/business-model/why-invest

In his book *Twitterville: How Businesses Can Thrive in the New Global Neighborhoods*, Shel Israel uses the phrase "lethal generosity" to refer to this competitive strategy of long-term, generous involvement in providing a societal benefit. "In social media the greatest influence invariably goes to the most generous participants, not the loudest," he writes. "So if you join a community where a competitor exists, or is free to join, and you give more to that community than the competitor, the other player is forced either to follow you or to abstain from participating in a place where customers spend time."34

Beth Kanter and Kami Huyse give us this concise definition: "Lethal Generosity is when a corporation applies its core competencies to advance social change in a way that contributes to business results and gives it a competitive advantage."35 In other words, Israel, Kanter, and Huyse believe that when a company leverages its assets for genuine social change, it annihilates competitors whose unique selling proposition is innovation or price alone.

Ordinary People as Change Agents

Another distinguishing characteristic of the social entrepreneur is its staffing with ordinary people. Most Fortune 500 corporations look for highly trained, professionally qualified people to manage their daily operations, while social entrepreneurs empower ordinary people to make an extraordinary impact on the world. Remember the potter in Nepal who became Village Forward's first contact in that country? He's still making pots…and serving as the organization's Technical and Training Director. He shows Nepalese youth how to make the filters on foot-driven pottery wheels and recruits village women to sell the filters door-to-door. (Of course, the social entrepreneur's customers are themselves making a difference, simply by being customers.)

We see a similar pattern in other social entrepreneurs. Edna Ruth Byler visited Puerto Rico in 1946 and witnessed the extreme poverty in that country, as well as the beautiful hand-crafts made by villagers there. Byler believed she could help them find a market for their products in the United States, and she started by selling handcrafted products out of the trunk of her car. She and other Mennonite church women eventually began a fair-trade cooperative called Ten Thousand Villages, which markets the crafts of villagers from around the world in 70 volunteer-staffed stores. Here's how they state their vision: "One day all artisans in the developing countries will earn a fair wage, be treated with dignity and respect and be able to live a life of dignity."[36] And they're well on their way. Sales topped $20 million in 2006 and Ten Thousand Villages was named one of the "World's Most Ethical Companies" by the Ethisphere Institute and *Forbes* Magazine for three years running (2008-2010). Ordinary people like Edna Ruth Byler are changing the quality of life of village artisans around the world.

You have noticed several common themes in the stories we have shared, so let's summarize these overarching values of social entrepreneurship. A social entrepreneur enterprise is…

Sustainable. Social entrepreneurs use renewable resources and avoid polluting the environment to help make the world ecologically sustainable. Sometimes they build a business on renewing clean water, clean air, and clean soil. They engineer their business processes to minimize their carbon footprint in the world, and harness renewable energy sources such as wind and solar to power their enterprises. They are equally commit-ted to economic sustainability. Instead of plodding a treadmill of endless fund-raising, they invest their money in activities that will generate profits for future operations. They pay fair wages to their employees to assure that they can live decently and sus-tain the daily work of the organization. Some have even limited top executive pay to a certain multiple of the lowest employee wage, to promote a sense of shared reward.

Even those who don't limit compensation recognize purpose above profit. These are often difficult words to hear in the mar-ketplace. And we are not suggesting that limiting profit elevates companies or individuals to a higher standard of integrity or anything like that. As a matter of fact, we don't know too many broke philanthropists; we aren't familiar with a slew of very broke people building hospitals. But what we are saying is that profit alone never can be the sole motive or the highest value of a significant enterprise. In his powerful book, *Good to Great*, Jim Collins shares attributes of companies that have become legendary. One of the shared values among each one of them – no exception – is that while profit was expected and pursued, each of the companies that have gone on to greatness valued purpose above profit.

Transformative. These organizations intend to change the world for the better. They expect to have a lasting impact on the lives of individuals, local communities, and nations. This translates into improving people's health conditions, providing educational opportunities, breaking down cultural barriers that hinder them, and employing them in meaningful daily work.

Social entrepreneurs are not interested in changing skylines with impressive corporate buildings. They want to change the social landscape of cities and villages everywhere, by liberating people from poverty, malnutrition, and disease for countless generations. Their most satisfying monument is a schoolyard full of smiling children or a village full of healthy families, gathered for their evening meal. That's the kind of change they strive for, year after year.

Visionary. Social entrepreneurs are not discouraged by the world as it is, because they set their sights on the world as it can be, on people working together for constructive change. What they're doing today seems small, compared to the changes wrought by marching armies and battalions of bulldozers, but they focus on the future significance of today's efforts. With every water filter they install, a family avoids dysentery and worse diseases. With every mosquito net they sell, a child avoids malaria. Each result may seem small, but the results are cumulative, and these entrepreneurs have the vision to see the ultimate consequences of their work.

Universal and varied. Social entrepreneurs can be found in every industry, from every background, and in any place. It is multi-cultural, cross-generational and bipartisan. When a social entrepreneur wants to change a country, he doesn't start with its president or prime minister; he starts with a potter, a weaver, or a farmer. Because of its cultural scope, this kind of business must engage people of all social and political strata. For this reason, a social entrepreneur is less likely to feel thwarted if bankers and political leaders are indifferent to the company's ideas at first. They will come around.

When national leaders support the work of a social entrepreneur, the business grows exponentially and is more likely to spread to neighboring regions. However, since a social enterprise doesn't depend on governmental subsidies or sponsorships, it is less likely to be disrupted by political upheavals, economic downturns, or natural disasters in a country. In most cases, such a business is operated by the poorest, least educated people of country — people who have learned to survive, regardless of what happens. Its universal constituency gives the social enterprise a resiliency that no other corporation can match.

Successful. Loyal customers, generous investors, and top-notch employees are drawn to social entrepreneurs because they want to be involved in growing, successful enterprises. These companies have limitless potential. As the world's population grows, we have a growing demand for food, clothing, shelter, clean water and air — indeed, for all of the things that social entrepreneurs produce.

A genuine commitment to social entrepreneurship "can lead to a true and defining differentiation from competitors," says Roy Sunderson of *Incentive* Magazine. "Your employees will feel it, and so will your suppliers, partners, and customers."[37]

When Community Loans of America decided to pursue purpose of profit, they began a search. Where did they want to begin? What mattered most to them? What resonated with their ownership, leadership and management? It didn't take long for them to form a consensus. Their hearts were with the children in the communities they served. Community Loans of America then formed a subsidiary, which they named Community Loans Cares. They then partnered with undefeated MMA fighter, and Champion of WWE's $1,000,000 Tough Enough Competition, Daniel Puder and his school mentoring / anti-bullying program called My Life My Power (more on My Life My Power later). Together, Community Loans Cares and My Life My Power are battling some of the most serious issues facing our neighborhoods. Teen suicides, high dropout rates, and a host of other challenges are a true threat to our communities.

The CEO of Community Loans of America, Bob Reich, isn't content with simply giving money. He goes in to the field with Daniel and sees the work in action. And he plans to go much deeper, involving their employees to help and volunteer with My Life My Power to become mentors in their neighborhood schools. This is the T3 culture in action.

T3 Corporate Culture

Holistic. Social entrepreneurs don't invest money alone in a cause they believe in; they pour their *time, talent,* and *treasure* into the effort-and they encourage their constituents to do the same. We call this a T3 Corporate Culture. Visit the web site of a strong social entrepreneur and you'll find a variety of opportunities to get involved in the cause they espouse. They ask stockholders and customers with specialized skills to donate that expertise to the effort. They even sponsor trips and short-term residencies in communities they intend to change, putting their people "on the ground" where they can make a difference.

They are taking a page out of IBM's corporate play book in this regard. IBM's Corporate Service Corps immerses its employees in the culture of a country where they plan to launch a new enterprise. IBM staffers live and work in that country for several months, applying their skills of management, marketing, or engineering to the problems of an indigenous company. By the end of their tenure, they've learned a great deal about the culture of the country and the unique needs of its people, so that IBM is better prepared to launch its own operation in that place.[38] Many start-up social entrepreneurs are doing the same on a smaller scale.

Later, we'll look at the T3 Corporate Culture in more detail. For now, note that a T3 company strives for total involvement (time, talent, and treasure) in the lives of the people it serves. Venture capitalist Catherine Rohr began such an enterprise after she toured a Texas prison in 2004. The inmates impressed Catherine with their resourcefulness and persistence — qualities that make great entrepreneurs — so she enlisted other business executives to teach them how to write a business plan and secure funding to start their own businesses. Catherine and her associates sponsored a competition in September of that year, where 55 inmates pitched their business plans to venture capitalists and several secured the funding they needed to launch a business when they were released from prison. Catherine and her husband sold their home in New York and moved to Texas to launch the Prison Entrepreneurship Program.

Graduates of the program have started 106 businesses to date, and PEP's 2011 annual report showed that 100 percent of its graduates secured employment within 90 days of leaving prison. Significantly, less than 5 percent of PEP graduates return to prison — compared to a recidivism rate of more than 25 percent in the overall Texas prison population. The program engages dozens of volunteer business executives who give their time, talent, and treasure to offer these inmates a new lease on life.[39] The *Wall Street Journal, NBC Nightly News, Inc Magazine*, and other national news media have featured this extraordinary business incubator, where the wholehearted commitment of community leaders has transformed other people's lives.

The Strategy of Social Entrepreneurs

Social entrepreneurs use a proven strategy to identify and meet the needs of other people. They use methods quite unlike the focus groups and online surveys that business schools teach you in Marketing 101.

First of all, *social entrepreneurs see their customers' problems firsthand.* Legendary in the annals of social entrepreneurship is the story of Professor Muhammad Yunus, who taught rural economics at the University of Chittagong in Bangladesh. Not content with textbook theories about the needs of rural people, Professor Yunus spent several months doing his own field research in 1976. He concluded that Bangladeshi villagers' greatest need was access to low-cost capital to start and sustain their own businesses, so he launched the Grameen Bank in the nearby village of Jobra. Functioning as a kind of economics lab for his students, Grameen Bank made microloans so peasants could start their own businesses. The professor told his students they could reverse the age-old cycle of low income, low savings, and low investment with a virtuous cycle of low income, injection of credit, investment, income, more investment, and more income.

And he was right. After three years, he interested the national bank of Bangladesh in his project, and they expanded it to other villages. In 1983, Grameen Bank received its independent charter from the government. Villagers are the only stockholders. By 2010, the bank had capital of nearly $1.5 billion (US dollars) and turned a profit of $10.75 million. [40] The 2006 Nobel Peace Prize went to Professor Yunus and the Grameen Bank. The Nobel Committee stated, "Every single individual on earth has both the potential and the right to live a decent life. Across cultures and civilizations, Yunus and Grameen Bank have shown that even the poorest of the poor can work to bring about their own development."[41] It all started because Dr. Yunus insisted on seeing his neighbors' problems for himself.

Second, *social entrepreneurs create solutions for their customers' problems.* Three young entrepreneurs launched a direct-sales skin-care company called Nu Skin in 1984, devoted to producing a high-quality natural product and attracting the best direct salespeople with strong financial incentives. The company's founders always wanted Nu Skin to be a force for good in the world and promoted a culture of giving. Nu Skin's 'force for good' brings the Nu Skin family of distributors, customers and employees in innovative efforts that multiply the company's ability to nourish and uplift children around the world. Nu Skin accomplishes this through the unique combination of three distinct approaches:

1. The Nourish the Children initiative, an innovative social enterprise providing millions of life-saving meals to the world's malnourished children.
2. The Nu Skin Force for Good Foundation, which provides grants to improve the lives of children offering hope for a life free from disease, illiteracy and poverty.
3. Community-based initiatives that ensure environmental responsibility and engage employees in meaningful humanitarian service with tangible and enduring results.

The Nourish the Children initiative combines the skills and resources of a for-profit company with the reach and heart of global, proven non-profit charities to nourish tens of thousands of children every month. How do they accomplish this?

Nu Skin manufactures and sells a highly nutritious food – VitaMeal® -- and allows distributors and customers to donate their purchase to charitable organizations that specialize in distributing food to alleviate famine and poverty. By donating a product, rather than cash, donors know exactly how their contribution is being used. Every VitaMeal donation reaches needy children through a select group of reputable relief agencies that frequently report on the progress and health of children nourished by the donations. Nu Skin provides incentives for commitments of ongoing VitaMeal donations and for encouraging others to join in donating millions of life-saving meals to malnourished children around the world.

Now check this out:

To date, **more than 300 million meals have been donated** since the program's inception in 2002. An average of 2.1 million meals is donated each month on an ongoing basis. In many cases, VitaMeal is served at school to attract children to nourish their minds, as well as their bodies.

VitaMeal plants in Malawi and China are providing jobs and economic development as well as nourishing food. These plants cut distribution costs, create a demand for cash crops and are improving the livelihood of many local farmers and local economies.

The VitaMeal story is wildly successful and typical of how social entrepreneurs address the needs of people they serve. They often seek the wisdom of the beneficiaries themselves, then use it to create an innovative, sustainable solution to a long-standing need.

Third, *social entrepreneurs tap into the passion of all their constituents* to power the transformation they want to accomplish. Blake Mycoskie, the founder of TOMS Shoes, was on a trip to Argentina in 2006 when he noticed that few school-aged children had shoes. A typical American tourist might say, "That's just how people live here," but Blake started asking questions of the children and their parents. They simply couldn't afford shoes, and children often missed school because of injuries or diseases of the feet, because they had to go barefoot everywhere. An idea dawned: What if TOMS Shoes donated a pair of shoes to these children for every pair their customers bought back in the United States? Soon there would be no barefoot children in Argentina.

Blake got excited, and he spread that excitement among his employees when he returned home. Soon thousands of pairs of canvas shoes were going to the children of Latin America, Africa, and other regions of the world. Enthused about these results, Blake began an eyewear company that did the same thing: A pair of eyeglasses goes to a needy child every time someone in America buys a pair of TOMS Eyewear.

TOMS Giving Trips now give the company's employees (and customers who win an annual contest) the opportunity to visit these locations for themselves and become part of the giving. The travelers return with a contagious zeal for giving, which attracts others to the work of TOMS.

TOMS has harnessed the zeal of their customers to be their champions in very powerful ways. We remember being on line at the movie theater in Southlake, TX, a very upscale area, and a women in front—dressed to the nines, hair perfect—was wearing a pair of TOMS. We commented, "Oh, you're wearing TOMS!"

Her response was fascinating. She immediately turned around with a grin that stretched ear-to-ear and said, "Yes, aren't they just so ugly?! But because I bought them, a child who couldn't afford shoes now has them." And she proceeded to tell us the TOMS story. Just think about that for a moment. Here was a woman who purposely wore shoes she considered unattractive just so she could tell a story of a for-profit company because it made her feel good! This is powerful marketing! (As an aside, neither we – nor we believe did she – regard her shoes as "ugly".)

Fourth, *social entrepreneurs incentivize people to meet the needs of the world.* Most people want to "do good" or "be neighborly," but seldom get involved in changing other people's lives. Social entrepreneurs use an amazing variety of lures and rewards to draw them into the action. Here are a couple of examples:

Hyper Island organizes events where people "can think and grow, using the transformative power of technology." They recently hosted a 4-day "Domestic Violence Think-In" for the International Rescue Committee, which brought together 450 students to create videos about domestic violence in developing countries. The students solicited ideas on Facebook, You Tube, and other media sites to produce 70 videos that the IRC is now using to spread its message on the same social media.[42] Their chief incentive was the opportunity to hang out with techno-geeks from 30 other countries for several days.

In 1992, Isaac Durojaiye began supplying mobile pay toilets for public events in Nigeria. Demand was high, so he hired a platoon of poor rural workers to build more of them. These people seldom had toilets in their own homes, so they struck a bargain: Isaac would provide the materials, they would provide the labor, and they split the income received at public events. Between times, employees of DMT Mobile Toilets park the johns-on-wheels at their own homes for personal use.[43] Their business is flourishing.

Social entrepreneurs know that money is seldom the best incentive, whether you wish to inspire greater excellence on the job or greater involvement in the needs of society.

5. Distinctive Attitudes, Common Myths

Nobel laureate Milton Friedman wrote an article for the *New York Magazine* in 1970 entitled, "The Social Responsibility of Business Is to Increase Its Profits." Social entrepreneurs agree with that idea, but they go farther. They desire to create wealth *and* social change, realizing that the more wealth they create, the greater impact they can have upon society in a sustainable way.

In fact, profit is a useful barometer of the social impact of the enterprise. As Jonathan Mariano explains, "The profit and loss of a business tells an owner how well (profit) or how poorly (loss) a business is meeting the needs of individuals in society."[44] Cause marketers pay close attention to the bottom line, because they can pursue their social mission only if they are financially sustainable. Fortunately, a significant number of consumers will pay "a socially-responsible premium" for the goods and services they provide,[45] which makes a profit more attainable.

Economic Sustainability

Paul Hawken learned this with the Smith & Hawken line of products for organic gardeners. These backyard garden enthusiasts are glad to pay a bit more for durable tools that were made in an environmentally responsible way. The Mennonite women who launched Ten Thousand Villages learned that customers will pay a bit more for authentic woolens made by the same people who raise the sheep, without any artificial dyes. Likewise for the purveyors of Fair Trade coffee, cocoa, and other consumer products that come from some of the poorest regions of the globe. According to Paul Rice, CEO of Fair Trade USA, "Through their conscious purchases, consumers tell companies that they care about the farmers and workers who produce their products. Fair Trade aims to address the underlying inequities caused by poverty and lack of access to market information that free trade ignores."[46]

In other words, consumers vote with their dollars in favor of products that are made with ecologically sustainable methods while paying employees a decent wage for their efforts. This market dynamic enables social entrepreneurs to achieve their objective of wealth *and* social change. So the *focus on financial sustainability* is a distinctive attitude of social entrepreneurs.

Global Transformation

Moreover, as their business grows, their social impact grows with it. After a career in political activism among migrant workers and operating a successful business as an I.T. contractor for government agencies, Juan Gutierrez was approached by the manager of an environmental consulting firm who wanted to take it independent from its parent company. Juan picks up the story:

> I discovered that both companies were in financial difficulty, but saw a great business opportunity. I took the risk and acquired [both companies]. I placed the

company into bankruptcy the next day and started rebuilding.

> Today, we have about 175 employees, five offices and various projects around the country and in Puerto Rico. Kemron cleans many types of contaminated sites. We helped clean the Hart Senate Office Building when anthrax was found there in 2001, and were involved in the cleanup of the BP oil spill in Louisiana and in the environmental cleanup in Mississippi after Hurricane Katrina.[47]

Environmental clean-up is a real growth industry. Kemron sees every new assignment not only as an attractive business opportunity, but as a step toward protecting our environmental future. Its growing business makes a growing impact in the world. This *focus on global transformation* is a distinctive attitude of social entrepreneurs.

Social entrepreneurs see potential where others see problems. Notice what Juan Gutierrez said about his decision to acquire two failing environmental firms: While anyone could see that these two companies were about to crash financially, Juan "saw a great business opportunity." He knew that America's demand for clean soil, clean water, and clean air would only increase in the years ahead. As a minority businessman, he knew that he had an advantage in bidding for Federal contracts. And he had learned how to care for the health and safety of his workers, through his work with migrant-worker activist groups. He was in the right place at the right time, with the skill and passion to make a real difference in our environment. So he stepped forward.

Opportunism with a Conscience

A similar story is told by Ray Anderson, the founder of Interface Global. In its first twenty years, his company became the world's largest manufacturer of flexible floor coverings for office buildings. While preparing a speech for a company meeting in 1994, Ray read Paul Hawken's book, *The Ecology of Commerce.* He describes that experience as "an epiphany," because he suddenly realized that a responsible company could be self-sustaining. Ray and his competitors have traditionally relied on limited natural resources: petroleum for plastic molding and manmade fibers, metal for modular frames and structural supports. As these natural resources become more scarce, that business model is doomed to fail. But when Ray caught the vision of a sustainable business, he realized they should use only renewable materials (wood, plant and animal fibers) and renewable energy sources (solar and wind) for the manufacturing process. Such a factory would be like a biological plant, using natural resources and natural energy to yield "fruit" for its customers — products that serve their immediate needs and be recycled into raw materials for their office needs in the future.

Interface Global's rivals see their industry as a zero-sum game, but Interface is making it a zero-loss game. In fact, they use the phrase "Mission Zero" to describe their ultimate goal, which is to have zero ecological footprint.

Most people read environmental forecasts with a sense of despair. Global warming, widespread pollution, and rapid population growth seem to spell disaster for Planet Earth. But social entrepreneurs like Juan Gutierrez and Ray Anderson read the same reports and ask, "How can we make a business out of this?" We might call this attitude *opportunism with a conscience.*

A focus on economic sustainability, a focus on global transformation, and opportunism with a conscience — these attitudes distinguish social entrepreneurs from the popular stereotype of "bleeding heart" activists. Yet other common myths cause prospective investors and employees to think twice about joining their cause:

Myth #1: Social entrepreneurs are anti-business. The American public has a stereotype of social activists like Erin Bronkovitch, whose zeal for reform trammels business with endless litigation and costly regulation. But social entrepreneurs are businesspeople themselves. They have stockholders and stakeholders to satisfy, and they are achieving profitability with excellence. A recent article in *Advertising Age* observed, "Socially conscious companies have stepped up their efforts with increasing effectiveness and productivity. It is an impressive movement and one that invites society at large to do even more."[48]

Myth #2: All social entrepreneurs are non-profits. The implication is that social entrepreneurs are out of touch with the realities of managing a business in the rough-and-tumble world where for-profit businesses must compete. However, all 25 finalists in *Business Week*'s 2012 "Most Promising Social Entrepreneurs of America" competition were for-profit businesses. Nearly all of the companies we cite in this book are for-profit companies, and some are quite large. (For example, at the end of 2010, Grameen Bank had deposits of USD $1.49 billion.)

Even non-profits can be self-sustaining. Visionary non-profits such as the Family Independence Initiative (which we'll examine in the next section) gladly receive donations, but don't depend on them for their future. So *non-profit* does not have to be a derogatory label.

Myth #3: We should let governments deal with social problems. We have tried to do this for generations, but government agencies scarcely make a dent in the needs. "Since 1965, this country has spent well over a trillion dollars providing services into our communities to address these issues that have all failed – the issues continue and grow in scale," according to the Center for Social-Profit Leadership. "Doing more of the same is obviously not the answer. A new approach is required if we are to have any impact on the social issues plaguing our communities."[49] Candidates in the 2012 Presidential Campaign promised that they knew how to provide essential social services while balancing the Federal budget, but the International Monetary Fund made a stark forecast: "The IMF estimates that fixing America's fiscal imbalance would require a 35% cut in all transfer payments [i.e., payments for entitlements such as Social Security and Medicare] and a 35% rise in all taxes — too big a pill for a creaky political system to swallow."[50] Clearly, these problems are too big for government agencies to handle.

Oakland, California, mayor Jerry Brown pitched the idea of the Family Independence Initiative to community activist Maurice Lim Miller in 2001. His idea was to gather several poor families in a cohort to help each other devise ways to lift themselves out of poverty. Each cohort received a token stipend to report their progress to the organization each month; but their real capital was their own ingenuity and mutual support. Here is how this self-determined "mobility" model departed from the "safety net" of government aid programs:

Mobility System	Safety Net System
Self-determined Path	**Prescribed Path**
Family acts on own goals and determines steps for self advancement	Family is directed by case managers or follows a process determined by a program
Reward Progress	**Penalize Progress**
Positive actions keep, or even increase, eligibility for resources	Access to benefits are reduced if the family makes progress
Families are Consumers	**Families are Cases**
Consumer feedback from low-income communities determines funding and policy	Funders' priorities and providers' feedback determine what services are available to low-income communities
Mutuality	**Dependency**
Family is expected and encouraged to share resources and assist others in community	Program is positioned as primary support of family inadvertently reducing the importance of peers and community
Families are Capable	**Families are Needy**
Families exercise control and choice, utilizing their strengths to act	Families are assumed to be in crisis and in need of outside help to make progress
Viral Spread via Role Models	**Limited Sustainability and Replication**
Relies on a few families to succeed in a way that inspires and informs other families	Expanding impact relies on continued funding and replicating entire service delivery apparatus

Copyright © 2012 Family Independence Initiative

"After two years, household incomes had increased 27 percent (excluding the payments offered by F.I.I.). People got promotions, pay raises, worked extra hours, and built up informal side businesses. After F.I.I.'s payments stopped, incomes continued to increase. After another year, they were 40 percent higher than the baseline."[51]   The Initiative is now an independent nonprofit with an annual budget of $2.5 million, yet it accomplishes far more in community betterment than government-sponsored programs that cost many times as much.

Myth #4: Charity is the solution to social problems.
Charities are not immune from the economic problems that face governments and for-profit corporations. When times are hard and money is scarce, people turn to charities for help — but that's when donations to charities decline, too. The British Broadcasting Corporation recently completed a major study entitled, "Charity: What Can We Learn from History?" The finding: British charities that were set up to meet social problems had to ask for government help in times of recession, in order to cover their shortfall of donation income. This led them to depend on government aid and eventually many of the charities were absorbed into government programs. Former President Bill Clinton notes that American charities try to fill the gap between what government and private enterprise do to address social problems, but by no means can they take the lead.[52]

Now and then, a news commentator dismisses the social entrepreneurship movement as a passing fad or idealistic dream. However, because the need for their goods and services is incredibly large and growing, the army of social entrepreneurs is growing, and investors are increasingly convinced that the future belongs to them.

In the next chapter, we will plunge deeper into the T3 corporate culture to understand why these organizations are so resilient and successful.

6. T3 Corporate Culture

Social entrepreneurship often begins with a company's CEO, but it cannot end there. It may involve the company's financial giving to a worthy cause, but it cannot be limited to that. As we saw earlier, true social entrepreneurship builds a holistic culture of change — a culture in which its people invest their *time*, *talent*, and *treasure* in a well-focused transformative cause. This T3 Corporate Culture is essential to achieving a social entrepreneur's objectives.

Sociologists have long recognized that a healthy corporate culture is critical to any company's future. Kim Cameron of the University of Michigan observes that corporate success "has less to do with market forces than company values; less to do with competitive positioning than personal beliefs; less to do with resource advantages than with vision. In fact, it is difficult to name a single highly successful company, one that is recognized as a leader in its industry, that does not have a distinctive, readily identifiable organizational culture."[53]

Cameron underscores the difference between a corporate *climate* and a corporate *culture*:

Climate refers to more temporary attitudes, feelings, and perceptions of individuals (Schneider, 1990). *Culture* is an enduring, slow to change, core characteristic of organizations; climate, because it is based on attitudes, can change quickly and dramatically. Culture refers to implicit, often indiscernible aspects of organizations; climate refers to more overt, observable attributes of organizations. Culture includes core values and consensual interpretations about how things are; climate includes individualistic perspectives that are modified frequently as situations change and new information is encountered.[54]

Get the picture? A corporation may have many different *climates* where a group has its own set of personal perspectives on the status of the company. There may be an upbeat, optimistic climate among workers on an auto assembly line but a foreboding climate in that company's boardroom. There may be a climate of warmth, hospitality, and generosity among a company's retail store staff while upstairs we find a climate of austerity in the company's accounting department. But a corporation's *culture* aligns the convictions of people throughout the organization with its purpose. What is the company about? What's it here for? What values will its people uphold, regardless of what happens to the economy or its own income statement? In a healthy corporate culture, everyone knows the answers to those questions, even if they cannot articulate them in so many words.

Innovation That Sustains or Tradition That Destroys?

A healthy corporate culture gives an organization "staying power," even when circumstances conspire to take it down. That has been the experience of Rob and Tara Hach, who started Anemometry Specialists, Inc., in northwest Iowa in 2003. The company measures wind speed for planning the installation of electric-generating turbines, a visionary business — so visionary that Rob and Tara were unable to borrow money from local banks. However, they persuaded the Small Business Administration to provide a $150,000 operating line of credit.

Their business doubled every year from 2004 to 2008. Even in the rock-bottom recession year of 2009, they kept on expanding. "We added a new office in Texas and hired four additional employees, bringing our total workforce to 30," Rob says. "We were able to avoid employee layoffs and maintain employee benefits."[55] They have installed more than eighteen hundred wind-monitoring stations in their first decade, some in remote locations that require workers to encamp for weeks at a time. Anemometry Specialists' T3 culture of promoting sustainable energy has enabled them to thrive in good times and bad.

On the other hand, imposing an inappropriate business strategy on a healthy corporate culture can have debilitating results. Atari emerged early as the leading developer of computer game software. The company achieved a creative synergy among its various programmers, who collaborated on new game design and sparked one another's creativity. Then the company hired a new CEO who had worked for a marketing company. "His cultural background told him that the way to run a company was to get a good individual incentive and career program going. Imagine his chagrin when he discovered a loosely organized bunch of engineers and programmers whose work was so seemingly disorganized that you could not even tell whom to reward for what!"[56]

His solution: He started an Engineer of the Month program to recognize the best game innovator of the lot. Morale collapsed, his best engineers left, and the company soon fell behind its competitors. "This leader did not understand a crucial element of the culture he was entering, so he made some decisions that changed a key element of that culture in a dysfunctional way."[57]

Atari is still in operation, though only a shadow of its former self. Its CEO told shareholders in his most recent annual report, "Our efforts have focused on execution and a strict investment discipline,…aiming to restore long-term profitability."[58]

Add a Cause or Change the Company?

Some companies court the favor of investors and customers by "adding a cause" to their business plan, but truly successful social entrepreneurs have a cause-focused culture. Everyone from the chairman of the board to the receptionist knows what their company is about, and they are fully invested in that purpose. They learn that when they give their time, talent, and treasure (T3) to the communities they serve, magic happens. This transformative nature of a T3 corporate culture is unlike any other.

In a T3 corporate culture, everyone can make a difference. Every person's gift is valued. When Blake Mycoskie takes a group of TOM Shoes employees on a giving trip, the team may include the company's custodian as well as its board chair. Each one brings personal compassion to the "front line," along with their vocational skills. Each personal contribution helps to transform the world around them.

In a T3 corporate culture, the lives of recipients are transformed. A woman who returned from one of TOMS giving trips said, "In Honduras, we met children who had never owned a pair of their own shoes before… I was instantly struck by the impact a pair of new shoes can bring … [The TOMS Giving Partner] explained to the children that the shoes would allow them to attend school safely and that they should work hard toward continuing their education, be proud of who they are and of their culture, and that they should do as much as they can to help their fellow citizens and community…The shoes become much more than just a pair of shoes; they represent a doorway into a new future with more opportunities."[59]

In a T3 corporate culture, the lives of givers are transformed. You can't miss this quote by TOMS Founder Blake Mycoskie on their website: "Giving is what fuels us. Giving is our future." Soon after he took his first group to Argentina for a "shoe drop" (distributing shoes to needy children), he reflected on this in an e-zine interview:

> The greatest thing about the shoe drop, and what has really inspired me to grow the concept even more, ... was the joy I would experience in seeing the people we took down there, like Missy, like Tej, like my parents, like my brother and sister, like my interns from this summer, and really seeing the change in their lives both during the trip and when they got back.

> ...It was so overwhelming to have all these people I cared about, who were dedicating their time and money to be down there to help me fulfill my dream of giving these shoes away, to see how touched they were and the joy they experienced in connecting with the kids. [That] was the most amazing byproduct of the whole thing.[60]

So the T3 corporate culture is all about enabling people to be change agents in the world. Sam Caster, the founder of Mannatech, says that "it is not about a company executive or a small group of people making a decision to change the world. By its very nature it includes everyone. Social Entrepreneurship links people from all over the world to the innovation that can create sustainable change. It unleashes human potential for doing well by doing good."[61] This is what attracts so many young Millennials to T3 organizations.

Let's examine T3 corporate culture more closely through the lens of Mannatech, a maker of nutritional supplements and skin-care products with revenues of more than $200 million a year. Established in 1994, Mannatech's products are "based on the premise that quality, natural health products can most effectively support the human body's natural inclination to stay healthy."[62] Mannatech sells its products through a network of local salespeople in 16 countries. Many of their customers sign up for an automatic order plan, which delivers supplements to their home (at a discount) every month. For each of these orders, Mannatech donates food supplements to malnourished children through its Give for Real program. A recent article in *Direct Selling News* explains:

> Mannatech's strategy is to take its Real Food Technology that it patented--vitamins and minerals and phytochemicals from real food sources — and put it in a powdered blend that allows other cultures around the world to blend it into food being cooked for children. In Guatemala,…that's black beans and tortillas. What the children receive is 100 percent of their micronutrition resources from real food sources.
>
> And what a difference it is making. The company recently sent a video crew to Mexico to document the progress made in the orphanages that received the supplements in December. What they found is that symptoms of malnutrition — the failure to thrive, the lack of appetite, the stunted growth, the learning disabilities and the bad behavior — have been alleviated. It does not take long for a child's body to respond to proper nutrition.[63]

Like most direct-selling companies, Mannatech provides generous financial incentives for its salespeople. However, Founder Sam Caster believes sales reps are attracted to the business more because it gives them an opportunity to improve the lives of needy children. "I think that has always been sort of the passion and the culture of our business — to change lives," he says. "And I believe if we commit ourselves to it, we will attract people from all over the world who are seeking a purpose-driven life."[64] Sam truly believes that giving changes everything.

For example, Don and Wendy Kremer of Colorado Springs came to Mannatech after they lost a 450-employee trucking business. "Now with no employees and just a cell phone and a laptop in our home, we are able to do more business and create more income for ourselves than we were ever able to do with that trucking business after 25 years," Wendy says.

Qualities of the T3 Culture

Don speaks of "the blessing that we get out of helping people. We have seen so many lives changed — physically, mentally, spiritually, socially. That's exciting stuff. We literally thank God every day for Mannatech."[65]

Notice the qualities of this company as its T3 corporate culture immerses its people in the business of changing others' lives for the better:

Compassion. Mannatech sales reps strive to meet the needs of people in several cultures simultaneously. Customers in the United States and other developed countries feel better and experience renewed energy by using Mannatech's nutrition supplements. Children in emerging countries enjoy better health by receiving the same nutrients in their daily diet.

Generosity. Mannatech rewards their sales reps financially, and demonstrates the importance of generosity by linking their customers with needy children. Again, it's a matter of culture. Mannatech investors, employees, and customers know that giving to others is "just how we do things."

Solidarity. Every time they eat a meal, Mannatech employees and customers share a meal with a less fortunate family. They are reminded in a very tangible way that they are part of a global community.

Servant Leadership. When company founder Sam Caster and his wife Linda established the Give for Real program, they established a corporate pattern of serving others. They continue to demonstrate that the quintessential Mannatech person is a servant of others.

Authentic Community. Mannatech employees describe a real sense of personal support from others in the corporate family.

In sales meetings, personal phone calls, and e-mail chats, they share their needs and challenges.

Transparency in Governance. The company's website provides full biographical data for each member of its executive leadership team and board of directors. The "Investor Relations" link provides not only the company's usual SEC filings, but also full documentation of its corporate governance philosophy, employee manuals, etc.

Purpose. The company's recruiting videos emphasize its purpose of improving the health of people around the world and affirm that every member of the Mannatech family advances this purpose. Here is the script from one of them:

> The desire for freedom
> Is one of the deepest needs
> > Of the human soul.
> No matter what your situation—
> Age, education, talents or abilities—
> > You have an opportunity in this life to choose.
> > Start small, think big.
> > Build and create something
> > > That did not exist before.
> > Do something of significance.
> > Enrich your quality of life.
> > Everyone can create.
> > You don't have to be an author, musician, or a scientist.
> > You don't need experience, position, or influence
> > In order to achieve something of substance and meaning.
>
> > You might say, "I'm not the creative type."
> > If that is how you feel, *think again.*

And remember, you are remarkable.
Think about it:
You are a master piece,
Created with beauty, function, and capacity
Beyond imagination.
With persistence, determination, and desire
You will make the world a better place.

Extend. Smile. Cultivate. Build. Develop. Start. Act.
The more you trust in yourself,
The greater your capacity
　　　To make a difference.[66]

The T3 corporate culture of Mannatech inspires its constituents to make a full commitment to global change. Fired with the company's vision, they intend to set the world aflame.

7. The Sustainability of *Global Cause Marketing*

G *lobal Cause Marketing* is integral to the sustainability revolution. Sociologist Andrés Edwards' groundbreaking 2005 study[67] remains the clearest guide to this phenomenon. Edwards explains:

> Sustainability encompasses a wide array of issues including: conservation, globalization, socially responsible investing, corporate reform, ecoliteracy, climate change, human rights, population growth, health, biodiversity, labor rights, social and environmental justice, local currency, conflict resolution, women's rights, public policy, trade and organic farming. These issues cross national boundaries, socioeconomic sectors and political systems, touching every facet of society and driven by life-affirming values that influence initiatives at the local, regional, national and international levels.[68]

Since it appears in so many different contexts, the issue of sustainability is bewildering. However, it comes into clearer focus as we retrace the history of this movement.

Sustainability activism originated in the environmentalist movement of the 1970s and 1980s. Soon after the United Nations appointed him head of the World Commission on Environment and Development, Gro Harlem Brundtland of Norway crafted a report entitled *Our Common Future*, in which he identified sustainable development as the goal of global environmental efforts. He described this as "development that meets the needs of the present without compromising the ability of future generations to meet their own needs."[69] *Our Common Future* recommended that any major development initiative be evaluated in terms of its impact on:

- Ecology/environment
- Economy/employment
- Equity/equality

Sustainability planners refer to these as "the three E's," and Brundtland's study saw a tight relationship between these three spheres. He insisted that it is futile to attempt innovation in one of these areas without changing the others as well. The United Nations' 1992 Conference on Environment and Development echoed this belief, declaring, "We can no longer think of environment and economic and social development as isolated fields."[70]

For example, if you devise a business plan that safeguards the natural environment in which you operate (the first "E") but does not generate enough income to acquire the equipment and infrastructure for your daily operations (the second "E") or pay your employees a livable wage (the third "E"), that business will not be sustainable. The same is true if you try to focus your corporate planning on any of the three "E's" and disregard the other two: Such a plan is not viable for the long term.

Stock analysts call these factors "the triple bottom line." In an article entitled, "Triple Bottom Line Scrutiny in the 21st

Century," the Motley Fool's Rosene Calvet observes, "Many investors believe companies that are good employers, environmental stewards, and corporate citizens will more likely prosper over the long term and be accepted by local communities... Major investment firms including ABN-AMRO, Schroders, T. Rowe Price, and Legg Mason subscribe to information on companies' social and environmental practices to help make investment decisions."[71] Sustainability — as measured by "the triple bottom line" — is becoming an important metric for investment decisions.

Edwards found remarkable similarity in the objectives of sustainability activists. Their groups are diverse in size, make-up, and leadership. They use different modes of operation to advance the causes they support. As corporate incarnations, they may be public or private firms, for-profit or nonprofit. Yet all of them recognize the interdependence of sound environmental, economic, and equity practices. In 2000, several groups crafted the Earth Charter, which states the aims of global sustainability with this Preamble:

> We stand at a critical moment in Earth's history, a time when humanity must choose its future. As the world becomes increasingly interdependent and fragile, the future at once holds great peril and great promise. To move forward we must recognize that in the midst of a magnificent diversity of cultures and life forms we are one human family and one Earth community with a common destiny. We must join together to bring forth a sustainable global society founded on respect for nature, universal human rights, economic justice, and a culture of peace. Towards this end, it is imperative that we, the peoples of the Earth, declare our responsibility to one another, to the greater community of life, and to future generations.[72]

Four Value Shifts in 21st Century Culture

Global Cause Marketers embrace this holistic worldview. They see their business pursuits as part of this larger effort to live as responsible world citizens. Edwards sees four important value shifts occurring as a result[73]:

1. *Prosperity.* The economy of a sustainable world does not measure prosperity in terms of manufactured goods, but by community well-being. Citizens no longer believe that the best neighbors are those with the biggest houses or the shiniest "toys," but those with the most healthy relationships.

2. *Ethical Responsibility.* The justice system of a sustainable world believes that to whom much is given, much should be required. To a lessening degree do courts hold governments and individuals responsible for righting the injustices of society. More and more, they hold corporations (the controllers of capital) responsible.

3. *Corporate Purpose.* Corporations are formed in a sustainable world to serve public interests, not private interests. Rather than seeing government agencies bail out troubled corporations, we will begin to see the opposite happen.

4. *Taxation.* A related shift has to do with the way taxes are levied in a sustainable world. Instead of taxing income and consumption, governments are taxing pollution and waste. Carbon taxes are a step in this direction.

Here we begin to see why Edwards calls the sustainability movement a "revolution." Such radical value shifts could affect every aspect of Western culture. If you have spent much time in Oriental cultures, you know that such values have been part of the Eastern way of thinking for centuries. Oriental thinking emphasizes community rather than the individual, shared prosperity rather than an accumulation of wealth by a few, and respect for the natural world rather than exploitation of it.

These values have been present in Western Judeo-Christian culture for two millennia because Jesus Christ taught them in his Sermon on the Mount (Matt. 5−7). President Barak

Obama drew attention to this in his "House Upon a Rock" speech at Georgetown University on April 14, 2009, in which he renounced an economic system that concentrates wealth in the hands of a few and impoverishes many, saying, "That's just not a sustainable model for long-term prosperity." Then he pointed to Jesus' parable of two builders:

> … The first built his house on a pile of sand, and it was soon destroyed when a storm hit. But the second is known as the wise man, for when "the rain descended, and the floods came, and the winds blew, and beat upon that house, it fell not: for it was founded upon a rock" [Matt. 7:24 – 25].

> "It was founded upon a rock." We cannot rebuild this economy on the same pile of sand. We must build our house upon a rock. We must lay a new foundation for growth and prosperity — a foundation that will move us from an era of borrow-and-spend to one where we save and invest; where we consume less at home and send more exports abroad.[74]

World leaders of other ideologies agree that we must make this shift in values to have a viable future. Former Soviet President Mikhail Gorbachev calls it "The New Path to Peace and Sustainability."[75] He says we cannot maintain peace by waging "preventive wars aimed at removing alleged threats," because "security in this new millennium is not just about protection from aggression, but also from disease, economic shocks and environmental degradation and resource scarcity." He concludes that global security in the twenty-first century depends on

> …developing, at all levels and in all spheres of life, a complex of attitudes, values, beliefs and patterns of behavior that promote not just the peaceful settlement

of conflict, but as well, the quest for mutual understanding, and opportunity for individuals to live har-
moniously with each other and the larger community
of life. Above all, it means promoting a new global
security and sustainability ethic.[76]

Gorbachev believes this vision of sustainability does not
replace the Sermon on the Mount or other religious teachings of
what constitutes an ideal world. Rather, it affirms them. Such an
ethic "asserts that real security and sustainability can only exist
in a world where finite ecological and economic resources are
protected in a spirit of stewardship to enable all to meet their
basic human needs and to live a life of material and spiritual
well-being."[77] Gorbachev has dedicated his life to this cause
since relinquishing the Soviet presidency in 1990. He helped
to draft the Earth Charter and in 2004 founded Green Cross
International, an ecological intervention agency modeled after
the Red Cross.

Biomimicry and Permaculture

The sustainability value shift can have a profound impact on
the way we create and operate businesses in the twenty-first
century. We get a hint of the possibilities as we explore the principles of *biomimicry* and *permaculture*.

Natural sciences writer Janine Benyus introduced the term
biomimicry with her 1997 book by that title: *Biomimicry: Innovation
Inspired by Nature.* She points out that human beings who seek
breakthrough solutions to their problems have often found inspiration in nature. We owe the invention of concrete, glass, the airplane,
and many other advances of civilization to scientists and engineers
who took time to observe the patterns of the natural world. Benyus
points out that nature has coped with environmental change for
billions of years, and we can learn much more from "organisms
casually performing feats we can only dream about."[78]

When rational business models reach their limits, biomimcry may come to the rescue. The textile industry provides a good illustration. Over the past quarter-millennium, garment-making has morphed from a cottage industry to a large-scale multinational enterprise that requires enormous capital investment. At the time of the American Revolution, every homemaker carded her own wool and flax, spun thread from it, and wove it into cloth. Now acres of sophisticated chemical equipment produce fiber from petroleum byproducts; giant textile mills with electric looms weave it into miles of fabric; and computer-driven robot assembly lines cut the fabric and stitch it together to create inexpensive clothing. The results: high oil prices, growing unemployment, and chrome racks of cheap clothes that fewer people can buy. Although rational business management pushes for greater economy of scale and lower cost per unit of output, this business model is not sustainable in the textile industry.

Nature will clothe organisms at the point of need, using materials that are readily available, and often fashioned by the organisms themselves. So how might an entrepreneur start a sustainable clothing enterprise using the principles of biomimicry?

It's not a simple matter of returning to cotton, the cheapest natural fiber, because cotton farmers use large amounts of herbicides and pesticides. We cannot use the vegetable dyes of colonial America because they don't hold up to modern laundry methods, and mordants (chemicals that cause dyes to set) are toxic. It makes sense for cottagers in other countries to raise, spin, and weave fabric for their own use—but transporting it to North American markets would require unsustainable amounts of energy and logistical effort.

Rose Gerstner wrestled with these dilemmas when starting her new apparel business, Sympatico Clothing. By using a blend of hemp and Tencel® (derived from eucalyptus fibers), she makes textiles that are soft and durable without using ecologically harmful chemicals. She employs a small team of home-based workers to cut and fabricate the clothes, paying them equitable wages. Her focus on sustainability even applies to the buttons, which are carved natural rosewood instead of stamped plastic or metal.

To accommodate women from a variety of cultures, Rose utilizes a "fit group" of diversely shaped women, "thus ensuring that the design concept actually works for the bodies of today's women."[79] This practice also ensures that a piece of clothing can be used for several years, even if a woman's form changes as she ages.

"As a woman with many years in the clothing industry, I am focused on creating beautiful apparel using earth-friendly fabrics in shapes designed for movement," Rose Gerstner says. "I want the clothes to be part of the artwork of your personal style. They must look good, feel good, be well made, and above all, reflect respect for our Earth."[80]

While Gerstner does not cite biomimicry as an intentional template for her business, we see these biomimicry principles expressed in Sympatico Clothing[81]:

- Nature uses only the energy it needs.
- Nature fits form to function.
- Nature recycles everything.
- Nature rewards cooperation.
- Nature banks on diversity.
- Nature demands local expertise.
- Nature curbs excesses from within.
- Nature taps the power of limits.

The Biomimicry 3.8 Institute helps corporations and government agencies to explore patterns of nature that suggest innovative ways to solve their problems. Many of their clients are start-up companies. You can browse several dozen projects under development at the Institute's research site, www. asknature.org, or watch Janine Benyus's TED video presentation of new inventions developed with biomimicry.[82]

Permaculture is a principle of agriculture that seeks to create a sustainable food supply by enhancing the economic and political culture of the community that uses it. As one advocate explains, "Self-reliance in food is meaningless unless people have access to land, information, and financial resources. So in recent years it has come to encompass appropriate legal and financial strategies, including strategies for land access, business structures, and regional self financing. This way it is a whole human system."[83]

Tasmanian educator Bill Mollison, who first articulated the concept, wrote that "permaculture is a philosophy of working with, rather than against nature; of protracted and thoughtful observation rather than protracted and thoughtless labor;...of looking at plants and animals in all their functions, rather than treating any area as a single-product system."[84] Aboriginal cultures had survived for centuries by following the principles of permaculture, which enabled them to support thriving populations with scarce resources.

Cause Marketers apply the principles of permaculture to the industrialized world with amazing results. For example, permaculture may be critical to revitalizing the City of Detroit.

Deserted by an auto industry that moved manufacturing operations offshore, Detroit's population has shrunk by more than half since 1950. The exodus out of Detroit has decimated the city's tax base, so that essential public services such as police and fire protection are being curtailed. Due to the city's high rate of unemployment and low median income, Detroiters pay a high portion of their annual income for food (third highest in the nation, after Boston and Los Angeles), while Detroit's obesity and malnutrition rates outstrip national averages. So city leaders decided to focus their attention on community food security. In November 2009, they formed the Detroit Food Policy Council, which articulated its vision in bold permaculture terms:

We envision a city of Detroit with a healthy, vibrant, hunger-free populace that has easy access to fresh produce and other healthy food choices; a city in which the residents are educated about healthy food choices, and understand their relationship to the food system; a city in which urban agriculture, composting and other sustainable practices contribute to its economic vitality; and a city in which all of its residents, workers, guests and visitors are treated with respect, justice and dignity by those from whom they obtain food.[85]

The Food Policy Council has revitalized the city market, established an adopt-a-lot program (which allows gardeners to use abandoned lots free of charge), and drafted the city's first agricultural use zoning law. "The farm can empower, drive the economy, reduce our carbon footprint and give us better food," says Council Chairman Malik Yakini.[86] Global Cause Marketers see a lot of opportunities in Detroit's burgeoning permaculture — among them the entrepreneurs who deploy fruit and vegetable trucks to city neighborhoods, supply fresh produce to city schools, and raise shrimp in urban aquafarms. Detroit must devise a host of creative strategies to solve the puzzle of its economic troubles, but permaculture is already a vital piece.

As sustainability entrepreneurs build networks for information-sharing, the pace of innovation increases. A quick tour of the Internet reveals scores of blogs, bulletin boards, and discussion groups devoted to sustainability, but here are a few worth watching:

The Global Transition to a New Economy (www.gtne.org) "maps innovative projects that challenge business as usual and contribute to the systemic change to our economy that we urgently require. "Sponsored by the New Economics Institute, which fosters the academic study of sustainability, GTNE identifies scores of Global Cause Marketers that have devoted their businesses to this effort — as well as sources of venture capital, government agencies, and citizen groups that support efforts to build a more sustainable future.

Imagination for People (www.imaginationforpeople.org) also attempts to identify, map, and connect a variety of socially responsible efforts around the globe, but with special emphasis on using artistic creativity to address societal problems. "The platform allows people working on projects to dialogue with the IP community and will soon enable them to submit calls for skills, visibility, connections and hardware solutions (open source hardware) at low costs. Disruptive techniques for facilitating collaborative working groups will allow the community to co-construct new 'resources' devoted to social innovation (methods, 'how-tos,' policy-making and collective challenges)."[87]

Of course, if your competitors are also striving to build sustainable enterprises, how will you prevail? As philosopher Peter M. Senge sees it, in the twenty-first century "the ability to learn faster than your competitors may be the only sustainable competitive advantage."[88]

8. T3 Cause Marketing

American Express coined the term "cause marketing" in 1983 to describe its campaign to restore the Statue of Liberty. For this monumental project, the company pledged a penny for every transaction and a dollar for every new American Express account that was opened during a four-month period. AE customers loved this patriotic campaign and promoted it by word of mouth, raising $1.75 million to give the American icon a new luster.

Since then, thousands of companies have undertaken some form of cause marketing. Edelman, the world's largest public-relations firm, reports that two-thirds of consumers believe "it's no longer enough for corporations to merely give money away, ...they must integrate good causes into their day-to-day business."[89] Successful cause marketers see significant increase in sales and profits when they champion the causes of their customers.

T3 corporations are especially proficient at cause marketing because their people live and breathe the causes they support. Indeed, T3 companies exist to meet specific needs they have targeted. At the same time they provide goods and services that enable people to thrive, they generate millions in profits to expand that support in the future.

Let's face it: Global needs cannot be met by government subsidy or aristocratic largesse; the needs are simply too great. We see it in the economic crisis of Greece and Spain, where unemployment now surpasses 25 percent, the worst peacetime record that industrialized nations have known since the Great Depression. We see it in the burgeoning health-care crisis of the United States, where some employees' benefit packages now exceed their take-home pay. We see it in large insurance companies' refusal to write homeowner policies in coastal states because they can no longer cover losses related to climate change.[90] There are practical limits to the taxes that governments can charge and donation levels that individuals can sustain.

But there is no limit to the potential profits of social entrepreneurs. "Many of today's entrepreneurs are building their businesses…on the idea of fulfilling a new kind of social contract," writes Ann Charles, "one in which organizations voluntarily take responsibility for the 'triple bottom line': people, planet, and profits."[91] This opens the door to some exciting new possibilities.

Think about it:

Since we can't *contribute* our way to a solution of our social problems, what if we could *consume* our way to it? What if our growing demand for food, clothing, shelter, and energy generated a growing cash flow to help the poor, homeless, malnourished people among us? This is the vision of social entrepreneurs. It's the story of hope that T3 corporations communicate through their cause marketing.

When consumers see that a company invests its time, talent and treasure to meet a massive human need, they want to become part of its story. They want to patronize its product and services to strengthen its societal impact. Cause marketing plays a vital role in this process. It identifies consumers most interested in a particular cause, and connects them with an organization devoted to that cause.

Compassionate Consumption

Imagine a world where consumers look for a "Compassionate Consumption" seal on the things they buy—a simple logo or symbol that says the company behind that product actively supports the community it serves. The result could be similar to what has happened since manufacturers began putting eco-friendly stickers on their products. (As we discussed earlier, the "green" claim is so effective in boosting sales that the Federal Trade Commission has established stringent guidelines for claiming that a product is eco-friendly.[92]) We've seen similar results with the fair-trade label for coffee, cocoa, sugar, and other products of farms in developing countries.[93] Given a choice between two competing products, consumers are more likely to buy one that represents "Compassionate Consumption," even if it costs a bit more.

If a consumer purchases a product or uses a service with the "Compassionate Consumption" seal, the transaction has a multiplier effect. The consumer receives a high-quality product made in an environmentally friendly way, while meeting the needs of people in distant countries, who can help their neighbors in turn. Traditional consumption depletes limited resources, generates toxic waste, and widens the cultural chasm between the "have's" and "have-not's" of our world. But Compassionate Consumption unleashes an amazing amount of human potential for good, like a nuclear chain reaction unlocks the potential in a tiny bit of metal to power a metropolis.

A Corporate Pledge

Let's pursue the vision a bit farther. It's reasonable to assume that companies using the "Compassionate Consumption" label would subscribe to certain standards, so that the public knows what they stand for. Here's what a "Compassionate Consumption" pledge might say:

- We give radically, live passionately, and create lives of impact, influence, success, and significance for every one of our employees and clients, as well as their clients and customers.

- We will help ordinary people make an extraordinary impact on their world. Whenever possible, we enable needy people to address their own needs, rather than making them dependent on financial aid.

- We focus on T3 principles in the conduct of our business. We teach our employees, customers, and investors to give their Time, Talent, and Treasure to improve the communities we serve.

These concise statements reveal that T3 marketers have a world view completely different from that of their competitors. Let's unpack each of them to see what they mean:

We give radically, live passionately... American Express started cause marketing by donating a *portion* of its income to a national cause, but that's not good enough for today's T3 marketers. They emphasize that the purpose of their entire business is giving to a cause. This is why Blake Mycoskie's corporate title is not Chief Executive Officer of TOMS, but Chief Shoe Giver. It's why Nu Skin describes itself as a "Force for Good" and Mannatech says it exists to help people "Live for Real...Give for Real." Here is how a recruiting video for Mannatech describes its business purpose:

There is value to life that goes beyond the things we work toward every day, beyond the rigors of the day-to-day grind — paying the bills, feeding the family, trying to get ahead. It is in small, simple moments we find this greater value...

- When someone shares a genuine smile
- When we see authenticity in a stranger's eyes
- When a friendly handshake guarantees honesty
- When we feel love laced with sincerity

- When you know the possibility in front of you is true.

These are the moments that make life real and give it real meaning. At Mannatech, understanding what makes life real is what makes us unique. We provide hope through technologies that radically change lives, products based on Real Food TechnologySM solutions that create results. We're a community of people with real passion for other people's well-being, focused on offering real possibilities for a better way of life. Our goal is simple…to help more people Live for Real.[94]

Giving is not a corporate byword, but the essence of what Mannatech does. Passionate generosity exudes from every statement of the 2-minute video. It's powerful T3 marketing.

We help ordinary people make an extraordinary impact on their world. T3 companies promote their employees' personal growth and direct involvement in global change. People work at these places not simply to earn a good salary with generous benefits; they work here to become better human beings and become directly involved in the corporate cause. Customers patronize these businesses because they know that every purchase helps to make the world a better place.

Family Christian Stores is America's largest chain of Christian retail stores, with nearly three hundred locations and five thousand employees. This private-stock corporation states its mission as follows:

Lord willing, Family Christian will be a world-impacting ministry and achieve business excellence. We exist to:

- Serve and glorify God

- Unite people and organizations in caring for orphans and widows
- Help people find, grow, share and celebrate their faith in Jesus Christ

Family Christian helps to reawaken and focus your heart and mind, giving you the courage and support you need to be the active hands and feet of God.

Family Christian carries out this purpose by sponsoring Good Goers Mission Adventure Trips. "It's not just a mission trip. It's a life mission." the Good Goers web banner says.[95] The company established a non-profit foundation, the James Fund, to coordinate these trips and distribute the company's donations to orphans and widows in the United States and several foreign countries. The James Fund has sent the stores' employees and vendors on 77 of these mission trips, donated more than $847,000 to adoption assistance agencies, and made matching grants of up to $8,000 in adoption assistance for each orphan adopted by Family Christian Stores employees.[96] A Family Christian employee writes, "We talk every single day, almost hourly, about how important saving lives are to us as a company. We exist to create families near and far!"[97]

We focus on T3 principles in the conduct of our business. Microchip manufacturer AMD realized it was not enough to issue a corporate statement of commitment to environmental sustainability; they needed to provide practical ways for employees to invest their time, talent, and treasure in the cause. AMD invites its employees to enroll in the company's Go Green initiative, which "embraces a lifestyle approach to environmental stewardship, promoting conservation onsite, at home, in the community and during commutes."[98] An AMD Green Team in Texas devised an "Energy Night Out" to find ways their community could conserve energy after business hours. Another team in India distributed reusable cups to employees and purchased bicycles to ride between buildings. A recent survey of the company's 10 Green Teams found that 98 percent of team members "agreed" or "strongly agreed" that "being able to contribute to a cause while at work improves their commitment to core job functions and to AMD."

Young professionals are attracted to T3 corporate culture because its employees enjoy a sense of personal significance in their daily work. The Cone Millennial Cause group interviewed 1,800 young adults (ages 18 to 25) and found that 80 percent of them want to work for a company that cares about how it influences society. "More than half said they would refuse to work for an irresponsible corporation."[99]

Likewise, T3 companies see the value of their employees approaching retirement. A consortium of social entrepreneurs in Europe has partnered with six E.U. governments to develop a program of financial education for their older employees. Some leading social entrepreneurs in Japan have begun a program of rehiring retirees, to make full use of their expertise.

T3 social entrepreneurs are also more likely to hire disabled people. Only 18 percent of disabled people in the United States are employed, yet they represent an enormous pool of unused talent—and passion.

Do Something Significant

Anecdotal evidence suggests that an increasing number of highly qualified people prefer to work for social entrepreneurs, even if they must take a pay cut to do so. They understand that success is what happens *to* you, while significance is what happens *through* you, and T3 companies offer employees a chance to do something of global significance.

This has always been integral to the American entrepreneurial mindset. The greatest legacy of well-known American industrialists has not been the corporate empires they built, but rather the way they improved the lives of everyday people. For example, Andrew Carnegie built the giant enterprise of U.S. Steel, but people remember him today for the network of public libraries he built to encourage public literacy and continuing education. Although Rockefeller constructed the monopoly of Standard Oil Company, people remember him for establishing the Rockefeller Foundation, which funded critical public health programs throughout the United States after World War I. Henry Ford's name appears on millions of automobiles around the world, not because he invented the machine (he didn't) but because his manufacturing and financing innovations made auto transportation available to working-class people. Although the fortunes of their corporate empires might wax and wane, these visionary business leaders wanted to be known for the "real and permanent good" they did with their fortunes.[100] Today's entrepreneurs want to do the same.

Daniel Puder is a clear-eyed, intense young man with spiked blond hair who intends to make a positive difference in the world. An undefeated Mixed Martial Arts fighter, Daniel could make a fortune from product endorsements and public appearances. Instead he focuses his efforts on an organization called My Life My Power, which he founded to combat bullying in public schools and after-school programs. He links arms with local law enforcement to sponsor local chapters of My Life My Power, where youth of all ages learn basic life skills and provide support for one another. The program addresses suicide and self-mutilation, substance abuse, teen pregnancy, obesity, and a constellation of other issues surrounding low self-esteem — which leads to bullying and teen violence.

Puder struggled with learning disabilities and obesity when he was growing up, and became a victim of bullying as a result. He wants to equip adolescents with knowledge and personal support so they don't have to endure the same kind of victimization. He now devotes his time to My Life My Power, and says the overall purpose of this business is "to make stronger and better communities as well as positively change the lives of our youth around the world."

"It gives me a lot more fulfillment in life just to be able to give back to kids every day," he said in a June 2012 interview. "I was in special ed. when I was a kid, so I know how some of these kids get picked on. It's great to be able to change kids' lives."[101] To learn more about Daniel and My Life My Power, including how to bring them to a school or after-school program in your area, go to www.mylifemypower.org.

This drive for significance is a common trait of today's entrepreneurs. Profit and prestige still motivate many people to take the risk of starting a new business; but these are not enough to sustain the marathon effort of establishing that business and making it thrive.

John Chappelear founded two businesses that grew to sales of more than fifty million dollars a year, yet he felt something vital was missing. "Most CEOs have the same symptoms I did," he recalls. "We have a gorgeous house, but are hardly around to enjoy it. We eat at private lunch clubs, but we're still hungry inside. Our expensive watches can't keep our time from slipping away.

"We have kids, but we may never really appreciate them. I didn't, either, until involuntary unemployment kept me home, instead of frantic and at the office."[102] Bankruptcy gave John what he calls "The Gift of Desperation" as he listened to friends who had also lost their jobs or businesses they owned. "Suddenly, they had begun to notice that there was more to life than profits and possessions," he recalls. "The horror of that experience became a gift to many who chose to see the lessons."[103] John began a business consultancy named Changing the Focus LLC, which helps individuals and companies find genuine satisfaction in life by putting work in its proper perspective.

Bonnie P. Wurzbacher is another executive who discerns the difference between business success and significance. A senior vice president at Coca-Cola, Bonnie began to see her work differently as the result of a sermon she heard several years ago. "It really struck a chord with me," she says. "I realized I had been searching for 'meaningful' work, rather than understanding that all work is important to God. To better understand God's purpose for business in this world, I began asking myself how my daily work honored God and others."[104]

As leader of Coca-Cola's global customer efforts, Bonnie is keenly aware of the company's societal impact. It contributes billions of dollars to the economies of twenty-six countries where it has more than a million employees. The company exerts a powerful force for good through its commitment to sustainability efforts such as developing clean-water systems, recycling beverage containers, and promoting the corporate leadership of indigenous workers. Bonnie says:

> Once I understood the difference my company made in the world, I could see how to be more intentional in bringing my abilities and experiences to my job. I also began to appreciate…that my work was an important way to impact the world for good. Once I saw my work from that perspective and understood God's purposes for it, I was able to see more clearly how to bring meaning to it.[105]

Publicize Your T3 Commitment

T3 marketing is critical to the success of any Global Cause Marketer. When customers, stockholders, and even employees see a company fully invested in making the world a better place to live, they respond with sacrificial commitment and loyalty.

This has been the experience of Arthur Ebeling, founder of a tea-based energy beverage company known as Warrior Energy. Ebeling was a star athlete in high school and college, so his company caters to athletes who want all-natural food and beverages for their training regimen. His company recently launched Lyme

Warrior, a program to educate the public about the debilitating illness known as Lyme disease.

"Tailoring specific cause marketing efforts to your business' customers can be an effective form of consumer outreach, as well as a means of evangelizing for your company's purpose," Ebeling wrote in *Forbes*. "…This cause bears personal relevance to me as I am afflicted with chronic Lyme disease. Using my business as a vehicle of outreach has helped to transmute my distress about the disease into a true sense of purpose in helping others combat it as well…Our Lyme Warrior program is focused on promulgating preventive education as well as lifestyle management for those who are afflicted."[106]

Lyme Warrior expresses the company's core purpose of promoting a healthy, all-natural lifestyle. It draws public attention, not only to vital information about this crippling disease, but also to the company's founder, who demonstrates that life can be robust and purposeful in spite of such problems.

Global Cause Marketing engages the public's imagination with your product, your company, and with you personally. It emphasizes that you are "all in this together," which is the essence of T3 *Global Cause Marketing*.

9. Investing in *Global Cause Marketing*

We have seen in previous chapters that *Global Cause Marketing* firms can be highly profitable and venture capital is flowing to them, along with the equity capital of unsophisticated stock investors. So why do investment experts express genuine surprise when they "discover" this trend, again and again?

We suspect the tendency to write off *Global Cause Marketing* is rooted in America's cultural myth about personal wealth. Investment advisers remember "robber barons" of the Gilded Age, who tried to "corner the market" on vital commodities in the late 1800s. But surely no one can "corner the market" on sustainable business practices; no one can build a monopoly on fair trade with craftsmen and farmers in the Third World. So how can anyone hope to gain a competitive business advantage, simply by doing what's right?

Another image seared into their memory is the wild-eyed stock speculator of the 1920s. Average citizens emptied their bank accounts to "take a flier" with volatile stocks, only to lose it all in the ruinous market reversal of October and November

1929. Why would anyone be so foolish as to put their life savings into start-up companies that make green products or loan money to street vendors in Bangladesh? Talk about speculation!

Yet another American myth about personal wealth is expressed in the adage, "If it seems to be too good to be true, it probably is!" We have seen too many get-rich-quick schemes on late-night TV, and we remember our grandparents' woeful tales of buying swamp land in Florida. So investment advisers fear that all this talk about investment opportunities in solar energy, flushless toilets, and affordable housing must be just that — talk!

Certainly, investors should be cautious. Prudent decisions require you to make a careful investigation of the facts. But there is such a thing as undue caution and unwarranted risk avoidance. If you sit on the sidelines, waiting for someone to eliminate all risk from the game and guarantee that you will recoup every investment in full, with interest, you will be waiting a very long time, so long that you may have to join the crowd that tears down goal posts for souvenirs.

On the other hand, if you take an objective view of what's happening in the marketplace, you will realize that *Global Cause Marketing* offers plenty of opportunities to invest with reasonable levels of risk. You can use proven research tools to assess those risks and anticipate opportunities where you can advance causes that are meaningful to you.

In this chapter, we will document the fact that "smart money" is shifting to *Global Cause Marketing*. We will highlight some research tools that investors use to make their decisions. Finally, we will examine how small investors can enter the ground floor of *Global Cause Marketing*.

Five Leading Examples

BusinessWeek magazine sponsors an annual competition to select the five leading social entrepreneurs in America. The list of 2012 winners is a snapshot of what's happening and a good indicator of why investors are attracted to this type of business:

1. The Paradigm Project sells clean-burning wood and charcoal stoves in Guatemala and Kenya, a business which has potential for strong growth and massive societal impact. More than 3 billion of the world's families cook over open fires, and the United Nations estimates that more than 2 million die each year of respiratory illnesses caused by inhaling the smoke of these household fires. Families in Africa and Asia spend more than one-quarter of their household income for wood to stoke their cook fires, and the incessant demand for fuel has stripped bare large tracts of the world's forests. In 2008, Paradigm Project founders Greg Spencer and Neil Bellefeuille conceived the idea of manufacturing a small metal "rocket stove" that would cut fuel consumption, reduce smoke and CO_2 emissions, and generate enough carbon-offset credits to pay for the stoves.

And that was the crux of their "paradigm shift": Instead of soliciting donations to buy stoves for needy families, they offered to sell equity in the company to investors, who could share the profits. Americans gave about $300 billion to charity in 2009, but invested nearly ten times as much—$2.5 *trillion*—in company stocks that same year. "Imagine drawing even a small portion of that money into social enterprise in the developing world, to invest in businesses that create social outcomes AND a profit for investors," Bellefeuille said.

The $40 rocket stoves are doing exactly that: They reduce household smoke by half, and reduce CO_2 emissions enough to earn about $95 per stove in annual carbon offsets. The company sold nearly forty thousand stoves by 2011, when corporate gross income topped $700,000. They have a goal of selling 5 million stoves by 2020.

"Could we be giving stoves away? Yes, we could," says Paradigm CEO Bellefeuille. "But that wouldn't last. Even if we raised enough donor money to give everyone in Kenya a stove, where would they go to get a replacement when it wore out? Or repairs when it broke? Or training?

"By selling the stoves, we can employ sales people and repair people and trainers, provide warranty service, and incentivize local partners to stay in the market over the long run because the business provides income for them and their families. We create an industry serving a real need. And we offer a product and service that we can be sure is truly valued — otherwise no one would pay for it."[107]

He concludes that "business is the most effective and efficient way to mobilize capital to solve problems in our world."[108] Clearly, his investors agree.

2. InterSchola of San Francisco sells surplus equipment from the city's public schools on eBay. Everything from old computers to cafeteria steam tables to road-weary school buses can fetch a bit of cash on the Internet auction site, so InterSchola retains a 35-percent fee and remits the rest to the schools. That has amounted to over fifteen million dollars in the past eight years, for items that school administrators used to pay salvage companies to haul away.

This company is the brainchild of Melissa Rich, an education-technology advisor for the venture capital firm Intel Capital. Her conversations with school officials revealed a need to convert idle assets into cash, so she drew up a business plan and gathered the first group of investors to launch InterSchola in 2004. She is proud of the fact that they weathered the recession of 2008–2009 and continued to grow.

"You have to have a business model for which there is a need," Rich said in a recent interview with the *San Francisco Business Times*. "…There was a very significant need that the customers didn't have the resources to do themselves. It has allowed us to survive and the need still remains."[109]

InterSchola's clients now include one-third of all school districts in California, plus clients in five other states, and its ten employees generated $3.3 million in sales for 2011. It was certified as a B Corp in January 2012, qualifying its investors for additional tax benefits.

3. Sseko Designs of Uganda has taken a unique feature of that country's public-education system and parleyed it into a thriving for-profit business. Uganda gives students a nine-month break between graduation from secondary school and enrollment in university, in order to raise money for their university expenses. However, Uganda's male-dominated society and war-fractured economy make it difficult for young women to find employment during this period.

With a graduate degree in communications, Liz Forkin Bohannan came to Uganda in 2008 to explore the idea of fundraising for a non-profit organization in that country. Instead she discovered a small community of women who had formed to train and guide each other through the nine-month transition to university. They had no marketable skills, so they eked out a living as best they could. Liz got the idea of teaching them to make sandals to earn money for their university education. Sseko Designs was born.

"We make beautiful things," Liz explains on the company's website.[110] "We laugh and we love and we dance and we learn. And every nine months, we let go and we send these incredible women off to pursue dreams of their own."

More than twenty women have completed the nine-month residency at Sseko and gone on to their university education. The company racked up sales of $430,000 in 2011, making it Uganda's largest exporter of shoes. They are now seeking retail partnerships around the world.

4. Retroficiency of Boston makes software that analyzes and regulates the energy consumption of large buildings, so that clients don't have to manually adjust thermostats or vents to achieve the greatest efficiency. When you consider the fact that the buildings account for 40 percent of all energy consumption in the United States, and property owners invest more than thirty billion dollars each year in energy efficiency upgrades, you realize that Retroficiency has great growth potential.

Founded by self-confessed computer geeks Bennett Fisher and Bryan Long, Retroficiency has analyzed the energy consumption of more than fifty million square feet of building space. Their primary clients are utility companies and property-management firms, although government agencies are also taking notice.

For example, Retroficiency identified $2.3 million of potential annual savings for the Liberty Property Trust by better regulating energy consumption at its 110 buildings. The entire assessment took less than a day, and did not require any site visits or hardware installations. Retroficiency then prioritized schedule changes and capital improvements that the company could make, by identifying which buildings offered the greatest savings.[111]

After raising $800,000 in venture capital for start-up costs in spring 2011, Retroficiency raised another $3.32 million that November to acquire the Clean Energy Services division of another Massachusetts company, Nextamp. This rapid build-out enabled the company to generate revenues of nearly half a million dollars in its first year.

5. InVenture makes online banking technology available to microbusinesses in the developing world. Entrepreneurs who start such businesses often have no bank account and are not considered creditworthy because of their low income and lack of business experience. InVenture bridges over that gap. By using the company's cell-phone application, the microbusiness entrepreneur can manage daily income and expenses "on the go." In the process, InVenture compiles a real-time credit score for the individual and builds a a bookkeeping trail that helps to secure financing. Potential investors and existing creditors can log onto the entrepreneur's account to view the current fiscal health of the business. Conversely, by tracking the patterns of visitor usage, InVenture can give the entrepreneur a list of prospective investors.

In other words, an entrepreneur's cell-phone application allows InVenture to serve as his electronic bank until traditional banks will assume the risk of a normal banking relationship.

InVenture was founded in 2008 by a young Columbia University graduate named Shivani Siroya, whose infectious enthusiasm attracts highly skilled professionals to the InVenture team. "While micro-credit has helped alleviate the struggle of subsistence living for many budding entrepreneurs in developing countries, it does little to expand these businesses beyond sole proprietorships and create jobs within the community," she says. "...Micro-lending's high interest rates, rigid payback structure and lack of guidance prevents micro-businesses from growing. They find themselves suddenly trapped in the 'missing middle': the gap in financial services between micro-loans and the traditional banking sector."[112] This is the niche that InVenture intends to fill.

Initial results are promising. Siroya reports that in the company's first full year of operation (2010), it matched investors with 36 micro-entrepreneurs in Mali, Ghana, India, and Mexico. All of them created jobs in their local communities, repaid their loan principal, and shared with investors their net profits of 15 percent or more. Each of these businesses also reinvested 5 percent of its net revenue in social initiatives to improve life in their communities.

Although these businesses are involved in a variety of industries and geographic locations, we can identify common themes in the way they operate. Each began on a very small scale, with one village or one client. They established personal connections between their investors, managers, and customers. (Their websites have a variety of video clips in which the founder, employees, and customers tell their own stories.) Visionary young people started them, in many cases immediately after they graduated from college. (None of the CEO's is over age 40.) And they immerse themselves in the cultures where they operate. Most of these 5 enterprises began with a visit to some foreign country, in which the founder's "culture shock" inspired the application of a new solution to a centuries-old problem. Quite often, to maintain this sense of heightened awareness, the founder settles in that country and becomes part of the community itself.

How Global Cause Marketers Use Their Wealth

While Global Cause Marketers are not shy about making profits or accumulating wealth, they use wealth differently than their predecessors did. Their values are radically different from those of commodity capitalists in the nineteenth and twentieth centuries. If you intend to become an active participant in *Global Cause Marketing*, either as an entrepreneur or an investor, you need to understand this tectonic shift in wealth philosophy. Here's how two Global Cause Marketers describe it:

> What we're building is a relationship economy, [based on] the accountability that comes from a relationship with another person, as opposed to a "one night stand" economy, where we don't have that accountability…Today, we don't know where our food comes from when it ends up on our plate, and what kind of impact it's had along the way. We don't know where our waste goes when we're done with that meal. When you put your money in a mutual fund, you don't know the impact of that money, circulating, where it's going. So we want to reconnect farmers with eaters, investors with entrepreneurs, and businesses with the communities and ecosystems that they serve. — Michelle Long[113]

> Today, we live in a money economy where we don't really depend on the gifts of anybody, but we buy everything. Therefore, we really don't need [a relationship with] anybody. If whoever grew my food, made my clothes or built my house were to die, of if I were to alienate them, that's OK. I can just pay somebody else to do it. It's really hard to create community if the underlying knowledge is, "We really don't need each other."…Only [the sharing of] creativity and gifts creates intimacy and connection. You have such gifts.

Just like every species has an important gift to give to an ecosystem, and the extinction of any species hurts everybody, the same is true of every person: You have a necessary and important gift to give...

An economist says essentially that "more for you is less for me," but the lover knows that "more for you is more for me, too." If you love somebody, then their happiness is your happiness, their pain is your pain. Your sense of self expands to include other beings...That's a different kind of revolution. There's no one to fight. There's no evil to fight. There is no "other" in this revolution. Everybody has a unique calling, and it's time to listen to that. That's really what the future is going to be. It's time to get ready for it, contribute to it, and make it happen. —Charles Eisenstein[114]

If you are an entrepreneur who hopes to attract cause marketing dollars to your enterprise, be sure your venture is dedicated to this objective of "profits with a purpose." Certainly, you can still find traditional venture capitalists who will commit their funds to you for a limited time, withdraw it with a healthy return, and go on to the next big thing. But if you want to court the attention of cause capitalists, expect them to get personally involved in your mission. They will not be "silent partners" by any means.

On the other hand, if you're an investor who wants to ride the wave of social entrepreneurship, be prepared for a deeper involvement than writing a check now and then. You will be invited to buy and promote the company's product, visit its customers, and get personally involved in solving their problems. Remember the T3 paradigm of social entrepreneurs; they expect you to invest your time, talent, and treasure in meeting the needs of the world. If you are not that passionate about getting involved in a cause, you will be more comfortable investing in traditional instruments (T-bills, bank CD's, etc.). Just be aware that the twenty-first century is leaving such passive investments in the rear-view mirror.

Two Pioneers of *Global Cause Marketing*

The pursuit of "profit with a purpose" is not an innovation of the twenty-first century. Although it is coming more clearly into focus now, we can see in retrospect that the most successful entrepreneurs and business tycoons of the twentieth century arrived at a similar philosophy.

Andrew Carnegie was one of America's most powerful businessmen at the turn of the last century. His Carnegie Steel Company perfected a method of producing large quantities of steel at an economical price, which enabled America to build the railroads, bridges, and skyscrapers that lifted the country out of a postwar depression. He sold his company in 1901 for $480 million (equivalent to $13.4 trillion in today's money), half of that going to Carnegie personally. He used the proceeds to continue his practice of building free public libraries, endowing public museums, and donating church organs to cities throughout America. In an article he wrote for the *North American Review,* he argued persuasively for earning "profit with a purpose":

> ...There is no mode of disposing of surplus wealth creditable to thoughtful and earnest men into whose hands it flows save by using it year by year for the general good...Men may die sharers in great business enterprises from which their capital cannot be or has not been withdrawn, and is left chiefly at death for public uses, yet the man who dies leaving behind many millions of available wealth, which was his to administer during life, will pass away "unwept, unhonored, and unsung," no matter to what uses he leaves the dross which he cannot take with him. Of

such as these the public verdict will then be: "The man who dies thus rich dies disgraced."[115]

Other business giants of the twentieth century have reached the same conclusion.

A more recent example is Richard M. DeVos, co-founder of the Amway Corporation. Richard and his buddy Jay Van Andel launched in 1959 to sell the first commercially available biodegradable cleaning solution, called L.O.C. (Liquid Organic Cleaner). DeVos says, "We were just two guys from Ada, Michigan, who wanted to have a business of our own. We were two kids who were hungry for success and who wanted to give others a chance to be in business for themselves, too."[116]

The duo marketed their product by word-of-mouth, building a network of individuals who contacted local schools, churches, and businesses to demonstrate L.O.C. and explain its benefits to the environment.

The company's product line expanded into nutritional supplements, skin-care products, and more. More than three million representatives now sell Amway products in 100 countries, generating sales of $10.9 billion in 2011.[117] *Internet Retailing* magazine has ranked the company #1 in internet sales of health and beauty products for the seventh consecutive year.[118]

Amway is still a family-owned company, now managed by the founder's sons, who continue to focus on improving the lives of their distributors and customers. President Doug DeVos says that Amway "offers a low-cost way for people to go into business for themselves. In the Amway business, relationships build an entire community that makes a real difference in people's lives." Besides giving individuals a chance to achieve greater financial stability, the company's network gathers support for key children's charities through its "One by One Campaign." Since 2003, this campaign has channeled $141 million to Easter Seals, Boys and Girls Clubs, and other children's causes. The DeVos and Van Andel family foundations underwrite similar causes, such as the 190-bed Helen DeVos

Children's Hospital, which grew out of a $50 million gift of the DeVos family.[119]

Global Cause Marketing in a New Century

Global Cause Marketers of the twenty-first century are personally involved in the causes they champion. This sets them apart from the philanthropists of past generations, and it inspires venture capitalists and conscientious investors to get involved, too. Leading investment advisors now counsel their clients to shift their money — and their personal involvement — to the work of Global Cause Marketers.

Senior investment analyst Pete Essele says, "…The practice of evaluating companies based on strong corporate governance standards, first-rate social practices, and clean environmental track records is becoming more mainstream. And as more and more investors become aware of such issues, we can only expect the ESG[120] space to continue to grow — and potentially provide investors with attractive investment returns."[121]

The Forum for Sustainable and Responsible Investment confirms this. Their 2012 report showed that investments in socially responsible firms had grown by 22 percent since 2009 to a total of $3.74 trillion.[122] To qualify as a sustainable and responsible investment, a company or mutual fund has to meet these criteria:

- *Screening* — The investment must meet basic ESG criteria. "Generally, sustainable and responsible investors seek to own profitable companies that make positive contributions to society. 'Buy' lists may include enterprises with, for example, good employer-employee relations, strong environmental practices, products that are safe and useful, and operations that respect human rights around the world."[123]

- *Shareholder Advocacy* — Shareholders are personally involved in promoting, delivering, or implementing the products and services of the organization. Shareholders also hold their corporate managers accountable for meeting the ESG standards they establish. "These efforts include talking (or 'dialoguing') with companies on issues of social, environmental or governance concerns. [It] also frequently involves filing, and co-filing shareholder resolutions on such topics as corporate governance, climate change, political contributions, gender/racial discrimination, pollution, problem labor practices and a host of other issues."[124]

- *Community Investing* — These companies store their capital in financial institutions that operate in underserved communities." Community investing provides access to credit, equity, capital, and basic banking products that these communities would otherwise lack."[125]

Simply put, enterprises that engage in socially responsible business will attract more capital. Investors see less risk here because these companies require less capital and, by definition, their principals have "skin in the game." They are more resilient in times of economic volatility because human need has no "downturns"; there's strong demand for what Global Cause Marketers do, in good times and bad.

Before You Invest…

This calls for a different kind of investment forecasting. The fund manager of a socially responsible fund or the stock analyst who focuses on T3 Global Cause Marketers cannot use the usual projections to assess the outlook of a cause-capital enterprise.

We met Jacqueline Novogratz of the Acumen Fund in Chapter 2. She knows this kind of evaluation can be done only in face-to-face conversation with the company's staff and customers. Here's how *Forbes* magazine described her recent visit to a gathering of Pakistani farmers, who operate with micro-loans from the National Rural Support Programme Bank:

> Suddenly the front door swings open and a tall woman with piercing blue eyes and brownish blonde hair struts in, dressed in a red tunic and baggy pants. Accompanied by the bank's president, ...Jacqueline Novogratz whips out her red notebook and gets down to business. "What kind of livestock do you have?" she asks one client. "How many male calves? How much money are you saving at the bank? What do you do with that cash?" An hour later, the notebook now filled with minute details of how, exactly, the farmers intend to pay back their loans, as well as whether their daughters go to school and what they want their children to do when they grow up, Novogratz walks out of the bank, satisfied. "I'm feeling optimistic about rural Pakistan," she tells me as a pickup truck loaded with field hands rumbles past a mosque. "Farmers are making good money."[126]

She wants to see how the lives of these borrowers are changing, because "progress is measured not in ROI but rather against the good that could have been done by simply giving the money away." Novogratz and other venture capitalists like her want to change the priorities of the people they serve, so that the impact of their investments continues to multiply.

When assessing the investment potential of a cause-capitalist firm, look beyond its balance sheet and cash-flow statement to its strategies and activities. If possible, visit with the principals of the company and some of the customers they serve, so you can see firsthand how the company is changing their lives. Several websites now evaluate the social effectiveness of American companies. Here are three:

www.goodguide.com – Primarily designed to help consumers evaluate the environmental, health, and social impacts of specific companies and their products, the Good Guide was established by U.C. Berkeley's Professor of Labor and Environmental Policy, Dara O'Rourke. The Good Guide has received favorable media coverage from *The New York Times, Newsweek, USA Today,* and other outlets. B Corp has certified the Good Guide as a "For Benefit" company.

www.bcorporation.net – B Lab is a non-profit organization that certifies whether a company operates "For Benefit" and not simply for profit. Many state and local governments now recognize this certification as a "B Corp" to be a requirement for favorable tax treatment when the company sells equities. Currently, more than 650 companies have earned the status of B Corp.

www.justmeans.com – A relatively new site, Just Means uses sophisticated web graphics to portray a company's performance as it is assessed by third-party rating services, such as the Social Responsibility Index (SRI) and Global Reporting Initiative (GRI). The aim of the subscription-based service is to give investors and corporate managers an easy way to assess a company's social impact.

You can be sure that other tools will become available in the near future, as interest in this economic model grows. You have a variety of decision-making resources at your disposal, whether you are a prospective social entrepreneur or an investor who wants to shift your assets to socially responsible companies.

10. Causes Worth Working For

As a social entrepreneur, you can choose to meet an endless variety of needs in your local community and around the world. Consider just a few possibilities:

Health and Wellness. Nu Skin and Mannatech have built multi-million-dollar businesses meeting these needs, but much remains to be done. What about providing advocacy services for hospice patients and the elderly? Postoperative counseling and support for bariatric bypass patients, who need to make a radical change of lifestyle?

Family, children, youth. Community Loans of America, through Community Loans Cares, has partnered with Daniel Puder and My Life My Power to take a stand against bullying and go to the front lines in the battles against teen suicides and a host of other challenges facing our children and our communities. Who will provide support to the families of autistic children? Software and training for parents who home-school their children? The issues, challenges and opportunities are endless.

Women's and minority needs. The recent economic downturn has hit women and minority groups especially hard, so unemployment among these groups is high and persistent. Juan Gutierrez's success in environmental services proves that there are special opportunities for minority businesses, in good times and bad. What others are waiting to be discovered?

Poverty and humanitarian aid (food, clothing and shelter). TOMS Shoes and other social entrepreneurs are accomplishing remarkable things in this area, but the need for humanitarian aid keeps growing, even in the industrialized world.

Environment. Interface Global, Anemometry Specialists, and other companies have brought innovative genius to the need for environmental sustainability. The relentless pressure of human development puts all of the world's ecosystem at risk, and with that risk comes new opportunity for social entrepreneurs.

Immigration. The recent Presidential campaign revealed the complexity of trying to address the needs of our immigrant families, both legal and illegal. What answers might social entre- preneurs provide?

Unemployment. Promises of full employment are peren- nial in the political arena, but this goal seems more elusive than ever. Non-profit organizations have launched a few bold experi- ments such as the Family Independence Initiative of Oakland, California. What other solutions might for-profit social entre- preneurs discover?

Education. We have a growing need to educate future genera- tions with the skills they need for the twenty-first century, and it's clear that government-sponsored public education cannot keep up. Michigan, Indiana, and several other states have encouraged social entrepreneurs to start charter schools — essentially, schools run as a business — and remarkable results are being seen.

Community Development. News media highlight the glar- ing needs of American cities: decaying infrastructure, declining tax base, and the exodus of essential businesses to the suburbs. Urban renewal programs have failed to stem the tide, but what might social entrepreneurs do to transform these urban ghost towns into new centers of vitality?

Look around you: What does the world need? What needs might you be able to fill? What kind of business would emerge if thousands of other people caught that vision with you?

Tens of thousands of companies inspire people to give their time, talent, and treasure to improve their communities and change the world. You could build a T3 company, too.

Can a Company Change?

You face more of a challenge if you already have a traditional firm and hope to move it into the cause marketing paradigm. Although it can be done, you may have to fight the inertia of being a business that's "Still Evolving, Now in Crisis." Such a business has survived its turbulent start-up phase and the founding entrepreneur decides to make a major change in its business philosophy. Theo J. van Dijk notes, "Considerable and sometimes critical changes are now required…Such a realization alone is a difficult notion to swallow for any entrepreneur and existing team. As an entrepreneur, you are not the most humble and patient of individual[s] and your personally picked team of employees soon grasps that what is required is not necessarily in their favor and often not to their liking." [127] Here are the most common objections you will hear from existing employees and business partners as you try to move from a traditional market-ing enterprise to a *Global Cause Marketing* shop:

"This will change everything. We'll be a different company." Don't laugh off this objection, because there's a lot of truth to it. This reorientation will require skill sets that your current team may not have or be willing to acquire—"people skills" that they didn't need before. It will set different priorities for your capital expenditures. It may mean that you have to abandon certain products and services that do not fit your company's new objec-tives. Change? Oh, yeah. There will be lots of change.

"Not all of us will agree on the cause." Again, that's a valid concern. Just as a *Global Cause Marketing* venture will attract people who have a passion for the cause you intend to support, it may alienate others. Not everyone believes that global warm-ing is real—and they'll pick a fight with anyone who does.

"It'll be hard to find enough employees to make this kind of commitment." This is probably the least of your worries. When word gets out that you plan to house the homeless of Detroit, you will be surprised how many qualified applicants will show up. Seriously, the next class of professionals who are about to get their degrees are eager to make their lives count for something meaningful, even if it means they have to start with low pay in a less-than-glamorous work environment. You'll have plenty of help.

"We can't afford to operate in such a highly regulated environment." We're likely to see more governmental regulation of all businesses, at least for the near future. These things tend to move in cycles, and we've just come through two decades of widespread deregulation, so the pendulum is about to swing back. If your cause has broad popular support, legislators will be more likely to accommodate you. In a highly regulated environment, your best asset will not be a shrewd attorney but a capable P.R. professional.

In that connection, a final word about marketing your new enterprise. Don't equate marketing with selling, because they are not the same. Selling is essentially one-way communication; it attempts to persuade you to buy my product or service. Marketing is two-way communication; it asks, "How can we make our lives better together?" That's the mindset of a cause marketer.

A T3 marketer comes alongside a potential customer, takes time to understand the customer's real need, and then enlists the customer's help in meeting that need. It's a form of community building, and that's what the global cause marketer wants to achieve. Visit the websites of TOMS Shoes, Sseko Designs, Mannatech, Nu Skin, and dozens of other global cause marketers. You will immediately meet the people who comprise their community, people who care for one another and strive to make the world a better place for everyone to share.

That's worth a hard day's work, don't you think?

Notes

1   "Chick-fil-A to Stop Funding Anti-Gay Groups," Michael Winter, USA Today
    OnDeadline, http://content.usatoday.com/communities/ondeadline/
    post/2012/09/19/chick-fil-a-money-anti-gay-equality/70000734/1, accessed
    October 18, 2012.
2   "The Best Eco-Friendly Water Bottles," Mikey Rox, Wise Bread, http://www.
    wisebread.com/the-best-eco-friendly-water-bottles, accessed October 18,
    2012.
3   Cited by Nancy Folbre, "The Profits of Virtue," New York Times, April 9, 2012.
4   Paul Whitford, "Smith & Hawken Founder Paul Hawken Believes that Business
    is Destroying the World," Fortune, May 1, 2002.
5   http://www.organicvalley.coop/about-us/overview/our-history, accessed
    October 18, 2012.
6   Kit Eaton, "Shopping Aggregators, Now with More Heart," Fast Company,
    March 10, 2012.
7   Stacy Perman, "Making a Profit and a Difference," Business Week, April 3,
    2009.
8   Helen Coster, "Can Venture Capital Save the World?" Forbes, November 30,
    2011.
9   http://causecapitalism.com/why-your-company-should-have-a-social-mission,
    accessed October 18, 2012.
10 Ron Silverblatt, "A Fresh Look at Socially Responsible Mutual Funds," Money,
    March 5, 2010.
11 "Sustainable and Responsible Investing Facts," http://ussif.org/resources/
    sriguide/srifacts.cfm, accessed October 19, 2012.
12 Aaron Douglass, "Marketing Malpractice and How to Avoid It," July 30, 2010,
    http://www.deepripples.com/blog/marketing-malpractice-and-how-to-avoid-it/

13 "Community Justice Division: Consumer and Environmental Protection Unit," http://www.sandiego.gov/cityattorney/divisions/communityjustice/cepu.shtml

14 Edward Wyatt, "F.T.C. Issues Guidelines for 'Eco-Friendly' Labels," New York Times, October 1, 2012.

15 Ibid.

16 "Greenwashing Litigation: A Growing Concern," from the July 2012 newsletter of Ice Miller LLP, http://www.icemiller.com/enewsletter/July09/Greenwash_Litigation.htm

17 http://www.greenwashingindex.com/about-greenwashing/

18 Clayton M. Christensen, Scott Cook, and Taddy Hall, "Marketing Malpractice: The Cause and the Cure," Harvard Business Review, December 2005, 83.

19 "Why Companies Can No Longer Afford to Avoid Their Social Responsibilities," Time, May 28, 2012.

20 Some companies call theirs a "corporate sustainability report," which ironically can be represented by the same acronym (CSR).

21 Michael Connor, "Nike: Corporate Responsibility 'At a Tipping Point," Business Ethics, January 24, 2010, http://business-ethics.com/2010/01/24/2154-nike-corporate-responsibility-at-a-tipping-point/#printpreview

22 Deloitte Development LLC, "Going from Good to Great: Making Your Sustainability Report Business-Critical," http://www.deloitte.com/view/en_US/us/Services/additional-services/deloitte-sustainability/8918785fc75b9310VgnVCM3000001c56f00aRCRD.htm

23 Matthew May, "B Corp ABC's," Venture Atlanta, http://ventureatlanta.org/2011/11/b-corp-abcs-with-matthew-may-partner-at-cherry-bekaert-holland-l-l-p/

24 "Chevron Assets Frozen in Argentina over Ecuador Case," The Economic Times, November 8, 2012.

25 Dave Bard, "Pew Applauds Largest Ever U.S. Court-Ordered Restitution in History of the Lacey Act," News Release from The Pew Charitable Trusts, August 20, 2012. http://www.pewenvironment.org/news-room/press-releases/pew-applauds-largest-ever-us-court-ordered-restitution-in-history-of-the-lacey-act-85899412212

26 Michael Adams, "Florida Approves State Farm 6.4% Homeowners Rate Increase," Insurance Journal, September 28, 2012.

27 Felicity Bsrringer, "Three States Tell Insurers to Disclose Responses to Climate Change," New York Times, February 1, 2012.

28 Ibid.

29 Cause Marketing Forum, "Statistics Every Cause Marketer Should Know," http://www.causemarketingforum.com/site/c.bkLUKcOTLkK4E/b.6448131/k.262B/Statistics_Every_Cause_Marketer_Should_Know.htm

30 Gheorge Militaru and Silvari Ionescu, "The Competitive Advantage of Corporate Social Responsibility," Scientific Bulletin, University Politehnica Bucharest, Vol. 68:2, 2006, 95–96.

31 "Refining 2012: Who Will Be in the Game?", Petroleum Industry Review, June 13, 2012.

32 "Warren Buffett, Bill Gates' 'Giving Pledge' Gets 11 More Billionaires to Pledge Their Wealth," The Huffington Post, September 19, 2012.

33 "Social Enterprise: A Manifesto," http://www.villageforward.org/about/manifesto, accessed October 19, 2012.

34 Shel Israel, Twitterville: How Businesses Can Thrive in the Global Neighborhoods (New York: Portfolio, 2009), 107.

35 Beth Kanter, "What Is Lethal Generosity?" http://beth.typepad.com/beths_blog/2010/04/lethal-generosity-defined.html

36 Creating Opportunities: Ten Thousand Villages Annual Report April 1, 2011-March 31, 2012, p. 3.

37 Roy Saunderson, "Top 10 Ways to Use CSR to Motivate Employees," Incentive, March 8, 2012.

38 Jeanne Meister, "Corporate Social Responsibility: A Lever for Employee Attraction and Engagement," Forbes, June 7, 2012.

39 "Prison Entrepreneurship Program FAQ," http://www.pep.org/who/faq.htm

40 http://www.grameen-info.org/index.php?option=com_content&task=view&id=39&Itemid=430, accessed October 12, 2012.

41 http://www.grameen-info.org/index.php?option=com_content&task=view&id=197&Itemid=197, accessed October 12, 2012.

42 http://vimeo.com/49343746, accessed October 20, 2012

43 Kattarina Sommerock, Social Entrepreneurship Business Models: Incentive Strategies to Catalyze Public Goods Provision (New York: Palgrave Macmillan, 2010), 4.

44 Jonathan Mariano, "In Defense of Increasing Profits as the Social Responsibility of Business," Triple Pundit, August 10, 2012.

45 Folbre, "The Profits of Virtue."

46 http://www.fairtradeusa.org/what-is-fair-trade/faq, accessed October 21, 2012.

47 Juan Gutierrez, "Cotton Fields and Brownfields," New York Times, April 14. 2012.

48 Bob Liodice, "10 Companies with Social Responsibility at the Core," Advertising Age, April 19, 2010.

49 http://socialprofitleadership.org, accessed October 21, 2012.

50 "Sponging Boomers," unsigned editorial in The Economist, September 29, 2012.

51 David Bornstein, "Out of Poverty, Family-Style," New York Times, July 14, 2011.

52 Bill Clinton, "Charity Needs Capitalism to Solve the World's Problems," Financial Times, January 20, 2012.

53 Kim Cameron, "A Process for Changing Organizational Culture" (Ann Arbor, Michigan: University of Michigan, 2004), p. 2.

54 Cameron, p. 3.

55 http://www.allbusiness.com/print/14601680-1-9a0bs.html, accessed October 23, 2012.

56 Edgar H. Schein, The Corporate Culture Survival Guide (Jossey-Bass, 2009), p. 7.

57 Schein, p. 8.

58   http://atari.com/sites/default/files/PressReleaseATAR%20FY11-12_FINAL-GB. pdf, accessed October 24, 2012.

59   http://www.toms.com/our-movement-shoe-trips, accessed October 12, 2012.

60   http://www.asitecalledfred.com/2006/12/08/10-quick-questions-blake-mycoskie-missy-peregrym, accessed October 24, 2012.

61   http://us.mannatech.com/social-entrepreneurship.html, accessed October 13, 2012.

62   http://ir.mannatech.com/phoenix.zhtml?c=62253&p=irol-homeProfile&t=&id=&, accessed October 24, 2012.

63   J.M. Emmert, "Mannatech's Give for Real Program," Direct Selling News, March 2011.

64   Ibid.

65   http://www.exploremannatech.com/successstories-kremer.htm, accessed October 24, 2012.

66   http://us.mannatech.com/company-on-a-mission.html, accessed October 24, 2012.

67   Andres R. Edwards, The Sustainability Revolution: Portrait of a Paradigm Shift (New York: New Society Publishers, 2005).

68   Ibid., 24.

69   The World Commission on Environment and Development, Our Common Future (New York: Oxford University Press, 1987), 45.

70   Edwards, 31.

71   Rosene Calvet, "Triple Bottom Line Scrutiny in the 21st Century," http://boards.fool.com/utx-21st-century-corporate-survival-pt-2-23658384. aspx?sort=postdate

72   See http://www.earthcharter.org/files/charter/charter.pdf

73   Edwards, 54–68.

74   Jesse Lee, "The Recovery Act: 'The House upon a Rock,'" White House web site, April 14, 2009. http://www.whitehousegov/blog/09/04/14/The-House-Upon-a-Rock

75   Mikhail Gorbachev, "The New Path to Peace and Sustainability," El Pais, January 24, 2004, http://www2.kenyon.edu/Depts/Religion/Fac/Adler/Reln481/Gorbachev-article.htm

76   Ibid.

77   Ibid.

78   Janine Benyus, Biomimicry: Innovation Inspired by Nature (New York: William Morrow, 2002), 6.

79   "Women's Hemp Clothing Moves into the Mainstream," http://www.sympaticoclothing.com/womens-hemp-clothing.html

80   Rose Gerstner, "About Sympatico," http://www.sympaticoclothing.com/about.html

81   Summarized by Edwards, 100.

82   http://www.ted.com/talks/janine_benyus_biomimicry_in_action.html

83   Katherine Wasser, "Permaculture: A Brief Introduction," http://www.permaculture.net/about/brief_introduction.html

84   http://www.permaculture.net/about/definitions.html

85 http://www.detroitfoodpolicycouncil.net/History.html

86 Quoted by Mark Bittman, "Imagining Detroit," New York Times, May 17, 2011.

87 "About Imagination for People," http://imaginationforpeople.org/en/discover-ip/aboutus/

88 Edwards, 52.

89 Cause Marketing Forum, "Statistics Every Cause Marketer Should Know," citing the 2009 Edelman goodpurpose™ Consumer Survey, http://www.causemarketingforum.com/site/c.bkLUKcOTLkK4E/b.6448131/k.262B/Statistics_Every_Cause_Marketer_Should_Know.htm, accessed October 12, 2012.

90 Andrew G. Simpson, "State Farm Pulling Out of Florida Property Insurance Market," Insurance Journal, January 29, 2009.

91 Ann Charles, "Opinion: Traditional Philanthropy Gives Way to a New Power," Business Ethics, October 15, 2010.

92 Edward Wyatt, "F.T.C. Issues New Guidelines for 'Eco-Friendly' Labels," New York Times, October 1, 2012.

93 Katie Gleason, "Study: Fair Trade Marketing Can Boost High-End Sales," Business Ethics, July 18, 2012.

94 http://link.videoplatform.limelight.com/media/?channelId=6725d108d8f344 94bace977d6663620a&width=640&height=360&playerForm=fd79f9fcc0914b 7ca2784cb863092920&deepLink=true&autoplay=true, accessed October 27, 2012.

95 http://goodgoers.com, accessed October 27, 2012.

96 http://www.jamesfund.org/fundraising-milestones, accessed October 27, 2012.

97 http://www.jamesfund.org/adoption-stories/the-adoption-of-our-daughter, accessed October 27, 2012.

98 Justin Murrill, "The Grassroots of Environmental Excellence at AMD," http://blogs.amd.com/corporate/2011/12/06/the-grassroots-of-environmental-excellence-at-amd, accessed October 27, 2012.

99 Jeanne Meister, "Corporate Social Responsibility: A Lever for Employee Attraction and Engagement," Forbes, June 7, 2012.

100 The phrase, "real and permanent good," comes from an essay by Andrew Carnegie in his book, The Gospel of Wealth. "One of the chief obstacles which a philanthropist meets in his efforts to do real and permanent good in this world is the practice of indiscriminate giving...," he wrote. —Andrew Carnegie, The Gospel of Wealth Essays and Other Writings (New York: Penguin Classics, 2006), 19.

101 "Around Town with Jen Meyers," June 8, 2012, http://www.youtube.com/watch?v=z62zej8KiYY

102 John Chappelear, "Profit from Life's Losses: Find Significance When Failure Happens." http://humanresources.about.com/od/healthsafetyandwellness/a/lifes_losses.htm

103 Ibid.

104 "Interview: Bonnie Wurzbacher," 4Word, November 30, 2011. http://www.4wordwomen.org/blog/2011/11/interview-bonnie-wurzbacher/

105 Ibid.

106 Arthur Ebeling, "5 Characteristics of a Successful Cause Marketing Campaign," Forbes, July 16, 2012.

107 "The Paradigm Project: Stoves, Carbon Credits, Profits and the Poor," Sustainable Business Forum, June 20, 2011. http://sustainablebusinessforum. com/marcgunther/52635/stoves-carbon-credits-profits-and-poor

108 Ibid.

109 Krystal Peak, "Entrepreneur Profile: Melissa Rich," San Francisco Business Times, July 22, 2011.

110 http://ssekodesigns.com/the-sseko-story/

111 "Retroficiency Remotely ID's $2.3m Potential Energy Savings for Liberty Property," September 20, 2012. http://www.environmentalleader.com/2012/09/20/ retroficiency-remotely-ids-2-3m-potential-energy-savings-for-liberty-property/

112 "Unreasonable Network: Shivani Siroya, Fellow 201. http://unreasonableinstitute.org/profile/ssiroya

113 "Fixing the Future," NOW, November 17, 2010. http://video.pbs.org/ video/1650808108

114 "Occupy Wall Street: The Revolution Is Love." http://www.youtube.com/ watch?v=BRtc-k6dhgs&feature=player_embedded#!

115 British Prime Minister William Gladstone was so impressed with this article that he arranged to have it reprinted in booklet form in Great Britain under the title, The Gospel of Wealth. It remains a classic in the literature of philanthropy. http://www.swarthmore.edu/SocSci/rbannis1/AIH19th/Carnegie.html

116 http://www.amway.com/about-amway/our-company/heritage/co-founders

117 "Amway Parent Surpasses USD $10.9 Billion in Sales," February 23, 2012. http://multivu.prnewswire.com/mnr/amway/49574/

118 "Amway Global #1 in Online Health and Beauty Sales for Seventh Consecutive Year," Internet Retailing, May 12, 2012. http://www.prnewswire.com/news-releases/amway-global-1-in-online-health--beauty-sales-for-seventh-consecutive-year---internet-retailer-93619239.html

119 "Helen DeVos Children's Hospital: History, Mission, Vision and Values." http://www.helendevoschildrens.org/ourhistorymissionvisionandvalues

120 This acronym stands for a company's Environmental, Social, and Corporate Governance performance. Investment advisors commonly use these metrics to compare the relative strength of cause capitalist ventures.

121 Peter Essele, "Socially Responsible Investment: From Fringe to Mainstream," October 2, 2012. http://seekingalpha.com/ article/899891-socially-responsible-investing-from-fringe-to-mainstream

122 "US Sustainable and Responsible Investing (SRI) Assets Up 22 Percent in Two Years," November 14, 2012. http://ussif.org/news/releases/pressrelease. cfm?id=196

123 "Sustainable and Responsible Investing Facts," The Forum for Sustainable and Responsible Investment. http://ussif.org/resources/sriguide/srifacts.cfm

124 Ibid.

125 Ibid.

126 Helen Coster, "Can Venture Capital Save the World?" Forbes, November 30, 2011.

127 Theo J. van Dijk, The Entrepreneur's Guide to Managing Growth and Handling Crises (New York: Praeger, 2007), 2.

Peter Hirsch, Social Entrepreneur

After graduating at the top of his class from Yeshiva University Cardozo School of Law in New York City where he was an Editor of The Law Review, Peter went to work with one of the nation's premier law firms, Cravath, Swaine and Moore. In 1992, Peter left the firm to work full time in sales and motivational training and corporate consulting. Peter has consulted for many Fortune 500 companies and sales organizations, developing commission structures, policies and procedures, communication systems and sales strategies. Additionally, through political and business relationships, Peter has helped a number of corporations establish markets throughout Latin America, Europe and Asia.

A passionate Social Entrepreneur, Peter is also a sought after inspirational speaker, delivering talks and trainings, ranging from keynote speeches, to full weekend trainings, to sales and motivational talks before audiences of up to 80,000 people. Over 1,000,000 lives have been impacted by Peter's messages on "Success by Design, not Delusion," "From Success to Significance," "Living the Significant Life," "From Motivation to Mobilization," "Communication for Transformation," "Whose Retirement is it Anyway," and "The Seven Secrets of the Money-Masters." His first four books, *Living with Passion, Success by Design, The Seven Secrets of the Money Masters* and *Living the Significant Life* have sold millions of copies in dozens of languages around the world.

Peter received his doctorate in ministry in 2001 and has developed leadership and mentoring programs for business leaders and pastors in dozens of nations throughout Africa, Asia and South America.

Peter and Bob are the cofounders of Global Cause Marketing, Inc. Learn more about the authors and their company at www.globalcausemarketing.com.

Bob Gordon

B orn in Providence Rhode Island the son of an advertising, radio and television executive. After graduating from the University of Miami Law School, Bob returned to his family roots and started from the bottom up in the advertising and film business. During his 38 years in the industry, Bob created and or filmed as a director/cinematographer many leading international global advertising campaigns for clients including Nike, Pepsi, Coke, Siemens, Heineken, SC Johnson, Chevy, Ford, Chrysler, Mountain Dew, Djarum, US Army, Chevron-Texaco, Exxon, Mobile, Bell, to name a few.

His campaigns have won many awards and have proven to be highly effective for clients. He has worked in nearly every phase in the advertising business, from creative director owning his own creative service company, upmarket, producer, film director and cinematographer. He created the first international commercials for brand Heineken. Sales rose as much as 40% after the launch of the campaign. Gordon produced the most successful launch of a new product in history with the launch of Diet Coke. He was tapped by Eastman Kodak to do the definitive film showcasing motion picture film. His work for brand Visa was chosen and is displayed in the permanent collection of advertising in the Museum of Modern Art in New York City.

Gordon brings a lifetime of work in all areas of traditional advertising to the table. He has seen the good, bad and ugly in the world of advertising. He helps us look into what the future holds for marketing based on what he has learned from the past. He discusses how companies can future-proof their corporate image to insure their legacy.